T0271706

About the Author

Clare Foges is a journalist and broadcaster. Previously she has been speechwriter to the mayor of London, chief speechwriter to the UK prime minister, a weekly columnist on *The Times* and a presenter on the talk-radio station, LBC. Between politics and journalism she has written picture books for pre-schoolers. She lives in Bristol with her husband and four children.

Clare Foges

The Paleo Life

Stone Age Wisdom for Modern Times

PIATKUS

PIATKUS

First published in Great Britain in 2024 by Piatkus

1 3 5 7 9 10 8 6 4 2

A CIP catalogue record for this book
is available from the British Library.

ISBN 978-0-349-43867-2

Typeset in Stone Serif by M Rules
Printed and bound in Great Britain by Clays Ltd, Elcograf S.p.A.

Papers used by Piatkus are from well-managed forests
and other responsible sources.

Piatkus
An imprint of
Little, Brown Book Group
Carmelite House
50 Victoria Embankment
London EC4Y 0DZ
An Hachette UK Company
www.hachette.co.uk

www.littlebrown.co.uk

For Mum, for everything

Contents

Introduction:
The Progress Paradox

It was not the diagnosis I had expected. Sitting in front of the psychiatrist, I could only hear him accuse me of being a reptile. I paid Harley Street prices for this?

A couple of weeks before, I had been hit by a panic attack so powerful that the floor of Oxford Circus tube station seemed to peel up and tilt towards me. Escaping to the street, ten-storey buildings became leaning towers of Pisa, teetering over the heads of workers scurrying into Pret a Manger for their duck hoisin wraps. The noise of cars and buses was sickening, the torrent of people dizzying. I fought the urge to lie on the street and stabilise myself by looking up at the clouds. A line from a poem floated into my consciousness: 'My mind's not right . . .'

So there I was, paying £220 for a consultation with a psychiatrist, when I heard him mention reptiles. I had wanted a diagnosis of generalised anxiety disorder and some pills. Instead, he was talking about my 'lizard brain'.

The lizard – or reptilian – brain is the most primitive part of our mind, a neurological fossil buried deep in the grey matter. It is the human brain's foundation stone, the part that governs all the life-sustaining processes we don't think about – digestion, heart rate, body temperature – as well as basic drives such as lust and hunger. Crucially, it controls our instinctive responses to danger, preparing the body to fight or run away.

The trouble with the reptilian brain is that it can be unsophisticated in responding to the modern world. It didn't get the memo that we are living in the 21st century, so when another part of the brain alerts it to a modern 'danger' – like a looming work deadline – it gears up the body as though it's facing an ancient danger, like a sabre-toothed tiger. Against a fanged beast, our best options were to fight or to flee, each requiring gallons of adrenaline. Even if the 'danger' is hardly life threatening, the reptilian brain still dutifully clicks the body into survival mode – cue galloping heartbeat and shortness of breath.

The doctor's neurological history lesson was a revelation. My heart-pounding horror on Oxford Street was linked to a nugget in my head that began its development between 250 and 500 million years ago, in the brains of fish that swam in the dark waters of prehistory.

'But surely,' I asked, 'our brains have changed a bit since then? Haven't they grown, got more sophisticated?'

'Well, the neocortex is more sophisticated, but it is still very old. The human brain hasn't changed that much in thirty, forty thousand years.'

Ping! It was a light-bulb moment, or perhaps a spark-from-the-campfire moment, for in that second the faces of our ancestors from forty millennia ago were illuminated, faces of those who didn't just live before us but who live *in* us, in the genetic inheritance that shapes our bodies and brains.

In this link to our ancient selves was the beginning of an answer to a question I had been asking since my teens: why am I so anxious? The feeling of having a boa constrictor coiled around my chest started when I was seventeen. Having a few alcopops would relax the snake for a bit but come the next morning he'd be vice-like around my ribcage again. One morning, after a particularly heavy night with that old charmer, Jack Daniels, I had my first panic attack. Pinned to the bed, my heart pounded so much that the sheets leapt. 'Mum, call an ambulance! I'm dying!'

Throughout my twenties the anxiety ebbed and flowed. Sometimes I was Zen, then work stress or a bout of comparing-and-despairing on social media would wake the boa constrictor from his slumber. Anxiousness drove me to drink like a fish and work like a lunatic. By my early thirties I was doing pretty well, on the outside: working as the chief speechwriter in 10 Downing Street, clocking off late and heading straight to a glamorous bar to drink espresso martinis until the last tube home.

Inside, though, I was jaded on a deep, deep level. In my worst periods – including a proper burnout – my brain felt as jagged as a bag of broken glass. I compared myself endlessly to other people: *She's written a novel at twenty-four?* I felt pummelled by

3

the implicit messages of our times: *Buy more things! Achieve more goals! Become more popular!*

When feeling panicky, I longed to switch off the noise: the ringing of telephones; the television news blaring in my office; the wailing sirens of the city. I'd lose hours on a website called private-islands.com, wondering if I could live off-grid on a two-acre chunk of rock in the Irish Sea.

It was as though the 21st century itself was jangling my nerves, so when the doctor spoke about how ancient our brains really are, it clarified a vague thought that had been floating at the margins of my consciousness for years: perhaps it's not my mind that is the enemy. Perhaps the real enemy is modern life?

That conversation with the psychiatrist sparked years of research into evolutionary psychology and the lives of hunter-gatherers. I don't claim to be an expert. I don't have a PhD in anthropology and have never spent months observing foragers in the rainforests of the Philippines or the valleys of Tanzania. I've learned through the writings of many brilliant anthropologists, archaeologists, evolutionary psychologists, scientists and historians – and what I've learned compels me to think that, as a species, we have travelled too far from the lives we evolved to lead.

To be clear: I don't want to turn the clock back to the Stone Age. There's a lot about life in the 21st century that I'm grateful for. I'm grateful for the medical technology that enabled us to see my daughter's brain when she was sick, for the drugs that boost my woefully underperforming thyroid gland, for the surgical advances that excised my mother's cancer. I'm grateful that infant mortality has fallen like a stone, that babies are born to those who once could never have had them, that we have globally agreed views on the basic rights that human beings should have. I'm grateful for false eyelashes, for ice cubes, for chickens with the giblets removed, for *Seinfeld* re-runs, streamed music, silk pyjamas, central heating. I'm grateful for the aeroplanes that have taken me to pink-skied Venice in the spring and scarlet-treed Vermont in the autumn.

Much of modern life is wonderful, *but* my research has convinced me that much of modern life is also jarring with our evolutionary inheritance – thus making us dissatisfied and depressed.

This realisation inspired fundamental changes to my own life. I don't claim to be 'cured' of all the ills and anxieties described above. Nor can anyone magic away all the difficulties and discontents that are part of being human. But living in a way that is guided by the lives of our ancestors has undoubtedly changed my life. It has released the boa constrictor from my chest, clarified what matters, and allowed me to be a better version of myself. It's called the Paleo Life, and here I want to share it with you.

Why do our hearts feel so bad?

At the turn of the millennium, the big song on the radio was Moby's 'Why Does My Heart Feel So Bad?'. It was a fitting anthem for the times. We in the West had never had it so good: the Berlin Wall behind us, no clash of nuclear empires to keep us awake at

3am; the 'end of history', they called it, in those years of relative optimism before 9/11. Living standards were rising, *Sex and the City*-inspired sisters were doin' it for themselves, our Nokia 3310s were making life a lot easier. We had never had it so good – so why did many hearts feel so bad?

Between the 1990s and the 2010s, the global prevalence of mental illnesses such as depression and anxiety surged.[1] In the UK, the amount of people with common mental-health problems rose 20 per cent over just a couple of decades.[2] Around one in four people living in England will experience a mental-health problem in a year, despite living in the sixth richest country on earth.[3] Some have called it the progress paradox: the more mankind advances materially and technologically, the worse many feel.

Why, despite the relative affluence and ease of our age, do so many feel so unhappy? There are many credible answers to this question: our work–life balance is out of whack; more families are breaking down; social media sucks us into a vortex of boasting and bickering; we've become disconnected from nature; we're not anchored by religion or ritual in the way we used to be; our diets are terrible; our sedentary lifestyles don't help.

Standing back from all these issues, a bigger picture emerges, a theme that joins the dots of our distress: as the world develops, billions of human beings are living in a way that evolution did not design us for.

We were not designed for working in brightly lit boxes for nine hours straight, for sitting down all day, for switching listlessly from the screen in our hand to the screen on our desk to the screen in our living room. We were not designed to live in competition with billions of other people, to fret endlessly about our future and how it might be better, glossier, richer than our past. We were not designed for mindlessly grazing on 'treats' that we treat ourselves to eight times a day. We were not designed to live hundreds or thousands of miles away from our friends and family, or for 'checking in' on our closest kith and kin once a month. We were not designed for vistas of concrete and advertising hoardings.

We were designed for a far simpler life, and one without a lot of the mental poisons that modernity and 'progress' have brought with them. We were designed for the life that human beings lived over the long millennia of prehistory, a life earthed by family, nature, purpose and the present moment. We were designed to be hunter-gatherers.

The long, long age of the hunter-gatherer

To understand the impact of our hunter-gatherer past on who we are now, it's important to understand just how long we were hunter-gatherers for. The agricultural revolution – which started to bring the days of hunting and foraging to an end for the vast majority of humans – began only around 12,000 years ago. In the sweeping span of human history, this is the blink of an eye. Before this, for 99.4 per cent of the time that creatures belonging to the genus *Homo* have walked the earth, we were hunter-gatherers of one variation or another. We have been settled, 'civilised' people for a tiny fraction of our time on earth: 0.6 per cent of it.

Let's put that 0.6 per cent into the context of a normal day. You rise at 6am, the darkness of your cave gently illuminated by the morning light. You spend the day foraging for berries, hunting and talking to your friends. As night falls you gather around the campfire for reflection and warmth, a huddle of familiar souls under an infinite sky. You fall into a reverie in the pall of camp smoke ... and then, at around eight minutes to midnight, you are suddenly teleported to Times Square, New York on the busiest evening of the year: your vision filled with flashing lights, towering buildings, people, people, people. Your ears are assaulted by the honking of taxi horns, your nose by the smell of greasy takeaways, cigarette smoke and exhaust fumes.

Those eight minutes at the end of the day would have been a huge shock to the system after the very different pace of life in the hours beforehand. This is not to suggest that prehistoric life was stress-free – facing the constant threat of attack by wild animals was hardly conducive to relaxation – but for millennia the rhythms of human life were markedly different.

Few people give much thought to the shock of this shift because, from an individual perspective, the changes have happened over a long period of time. But it is bred in our bones – and our minds – to live differently from the way we do now. Forty thousand years ago we might have met a few hundred people in a lifetime; today it's countless thousands. Back then we were only required to care about what directly affected us; now the news plugs our emotions into the agonies and sufferings of the world. Back then we had a daily practical purpose – to find and feed – now we're endlessly searching for distraction and dopamine hits.

'The human brain hasn't changed that much in thirty, forty thousand years . . .' No wonder we're burned out.

Fixing our environment, not just our brains

I am hardly the first person to point out that the mismatch between our Stone Age brains and our modern environment is making us sick. A whole conference hall of evolutionary psychologists could tell you that. But the remedy for that sickness is usually to focus on calming our fretful minds through deep breathing, mindfulness, meditation, and so on.

I'm not knocking these tools – they are proven anxiety-helpers – but they treat the symptoms of our malaise rather than its cause. They 'fix' our ancient minds in order that they can cope better with modern life. Why don't we reverse this, and fix the aspects of modern life that aren't working for us, too?

You may have heard of the hugely popular Paleo diet, based on the simple idea that our guts – which evolved a long time ago – are better able to digest the kind of foods we ate a long time ago: plants and simple proteins, not Big Macs and microwave meals. The Paleo diet doesn't suggest that we simply mitigate against the effects of modern food by taking a probiotic; it suggests we rewind the clock to more digestible foods. Paleo Life applies the same principle to our minds: adapting our lifestyle so that it is kinder to our ancient brains.

In this book is a programme of practical ideas to tailor our 21st-century environment to our Paleo brains. This isn't about going all Flintstones; no one wants to say goodbye to deodorant or 400-thread-count sheets. Instead, we'll explore why we should be more discerning about which of the trends and teachings of today we allow into our lives, and how we can imitate some of the patterns followed by our hunter-gatherer forebears.

Crank your mind open, because this book will upend a lot of what you have been told is true. You have learned that being a successful human means being super-popular, ultra-busy, engaged with the world. The Paleo Life will suggest that a lot of the beliefs we've been sucked into are actually doing us harm, making us wired, tired and jaded.

Please don't treat this as a rule book. They never work. Think of it instead as a rail book: laying down some tracks to guide us on a different, more fulfilling journey. It's not just a journey away from the damaging elements of modern life; it's a journey back to ourselves. The goal: to live in a way that is more fully, contentedly, simply, human.

We can't stop the modern world and get off, but we can take steps to better enjoy the ride.

1

Meet the Hunter-Gatherers

The artist steps into the cave. In his hand is a grease lamp made of limestone, its indentations holding bone marrow that has been lit to cast a pool of golden light on the walls around. Making his way through the gloom, the artist climbs the wooden scaffold until he is inches from the cave ceiling. There he sweeps a piece of dampened moss through a pile of clay ochre and begins to paint the forelock of a horse, its long, graceful nose and eyes.

Seventeen thousand years later, another artist stepped out of the northern Spanish cave and into the dazzling sunlight. 'Well, what did you think?' asked his guide. Pablo Picasso shook his head in amazement: 'Seventeen thousand years, and we have invented nothing!'

Perhaps he had expected to see the daubings of a savage. Instead, Picasso looked at the brushstrokes of a 17,000-year-old distant peer and felt the thrill of recognition. These were not savages. They created. They dreamed. 'They' were us.

Cave paintings are magical because they capture the moment

in prehistory when human intelligence exploded into something powerful and wonderful, becoming the force that would eventually bring us Angkor Wat and 'Ave Maria', flight and nuclear fission, pyramids and Pythagoras' theorem, democracy and the declaration of human rights. The great flowering of human creativity and ingenuity began in those caves.

Cave art isn't the beginning of the tale, however. The story of humans began a long time before anyone mashed up some clay and water to paint a mammoth. If you were to climb into a time machine and land in sub-Saharan eastern Africa 2.5 million years ago, you might meet some creatures who looked somewhat like us; hairier and rather ape-like, yes, but able to walk upright: *Homo habilis*, the first of the genus 'Homo'.

Around two million years ago came the evolution of *Homo erectus,* whose brains were significantly larger than those of *Homo habilis*. Perhaps in that extra brainpower there was the first spark of human curiosity, for *Homo erectus* were the first brave humans to strike out of their African homeland.

Armed with sharpened stone hand axes with which to rip up the carcasses of deer – or even hippos – on their way, over a period of 1.75 million years *Homo erectus* spread out and up through Africa, crossed through the modern-day Middle East and the Gulf into West and East Asia, all the way to the land now known as Indonesia.

Because the traits needed to survive snowy tundras are different from those needed on swampy islands, different species evolved, so that by 300,000 years ago nine different kinds of human walked the earth at the same time. On the baking savannahs of central Africa lived *Homo rhodesiensis*; in the tropics of South-East Asia *H. erectus*; on the islands of Indonesia the diminutive *Homo floresiensis* and in the woodlands of Europe *Homo neanderthalis*.

Eventually, around 200,000 years ago, a species evolved in Africa that would go on to conquer and dominate the world: our own *Homo sapiens*.

What we know of our ancestors

Paleolithic archaeology is a detective story, not a whodunnit but a howdunnit: how did our ancestors live, work, eat, fight, trade, die? There are limits as to what we can know, of course, but using bones and artefacts scattered from Australia to Zimbabwe we can partially draw back the dark, heavy veil of prehistory.

What do we know of the early *Homo sapiens*? We know that they used teardrop-shaped stone hand axes and throwing spears to ambush and kill antelopes, gazelles, wildebeests and other large animals. The discovery of stone-tipped arrows and bows in Sibudu Cave in South Africa suggests that by 62,000 BCE many had discovered a new way to kill. When prey eluded the arrow, they foraged for berries, plants, nuts and seeds.

Twenty-thousand-year-old fishing hooks found in a cave in East Timor suggest that some of them were casting lines for fish, too. Perhaps these were caught from a boat or raft; although the remains of a wooden vessel would be unlikely to last in the soil for millennia, we can be pretty confident that early humans were seafaring, for how else would they have made it to islands such as Crete or Indonesia? When the catch was brought home, it was probably cooked on a fire, for humans have heated food in this way for almost 800,000 years, and quite possibly longer.

We know that most early *Homo sapiens* lived in bands of around thirty to fifty people, and – judging by the state of some of the skeletons found – we can be pretty sure that the sick and vulnerable were cared for. In 2022 archaeologists working in a remote part of Indonesian Borneo found the remains of a young hunter-gatherer who had lived 31,000 years before. They found an astounding detail: his lower left leg had been surgically amputated. Whether wide awake or sedated with some natural concoction, the patient had endured the agony of having his leg sawn off with a sharpened stone. While we might have imagined that blood loss or infection would have seen him off pretty swiftly, this hunter-gatherer survived for years after the surgery. How? Only with the care of his tribe.

We know that thousands of years before the invention of the wheel, hunter-gatherers were rolling and pinching coils of clay, shaping them into vessels and baking them for use as cups, bowls and storage; a haul of ceramic fragments found in China dates back 20,000 years.

We know – thanks to the remarkable efforts of scientists who have studied the genetic lineage of clothes lice – that about 170,000 years ago, humans started wearing garments. At first these were just animal hides worn as shawls. By around 43,000 BCE, humans in what is now Siberia and China had developed eye sewing needles sharp enough to pierce a hide. Needles have been found all over the world, from Wyoming to Western Europe, meaning that these very helpful inventions were developed in isolation.

There is evidence that early humans wore clothes not only to stay warm but to look good, too: tiny pierced shells found on the body of a child who lived 12,000 years ago suggest that they were sewn on to the clothing. A thirty-three-shell bead necklace found in Morocco conjures up who might have worn it: pale shells against dark skin, a woman enjoying the power that youth and beauty bestowed on her.

We know they made music. Inside the dank, dark Hohle Fels cave in south-west Germany archaeologists found the world's oldest musical instruments: 43,000-year-old bone flutes made of vulture wing and mammoth tusk. Not only did our ancestors enjoy making and listening to music, they also had the time to halve the bones, whittle them down, pierce holes in them and create a sealant to stick the halves back together. The location of these flutes – found near to hearths inside the cave – suggests that then, as now, we liked to listen to music together.

We know they loved, cherished and grieved accordingly. Ornate burial sites, such as that at Sunghir, 200 kilometres east of modern-day Moscow, show how some hunter-gatherers were sent to the next life amid a trove of treasures: mammoth ivory beads, pierced fox canines, ivory armbands.

Perhaps the most affecting human burial is the oldest (that we know of), discovered in Kenya's Panga ya Saidi cave in 2021. A toddler who lived around 80,000 years ago is curled on his side. From the way the skeleton has crumbled, scientists deduce that a pillow made of leaves or animal hide was placed under his head. In this sad detail eighty millennia are crunched down to nothing. We grieve with those who grieved; the mother tucking a pillow under her baby's head to ensure his comfort in the next life.

The clearest glimpses of ancient life come from cave paintings, protected from millennia of storms and sweltering summers. One of the most famous is the Bird Man of Lascaux in France, a strange sketch of a man falling backwards, his erect penis pointing at a bison charging towards him. What is notable about this man, aside from the erection, is that he has the head of a bird. To the 21st-century mind accustomed to CGI graphics, this is hardly mind-blowing, but it is important to the human story.

Bird men have never existed, meaning that *Homo sapiens* could *imagine* things. When you can imagine, you can talk and think about things that don't actually exist, and these things – religion, myths, legends, fantasies, and even nations – can motivate and inspire vast numbers of people to collaborate together on common goals. In short, imagination is how we became the most spectacularly successful species the world has ever seen.

'Nasty, brutish and short'?

This much we know: our ancestors thought with complexity, loved with sincerity, hunted with dexterity, lived in community, indulged in creativity. But given the goal of the Paleo Life is to improve our wellbeing, you might be thinking: *Yes, but did they live more contentedly?*

Alas, the human skull is no black box from which we can learn the joys and sorrows that were contained within it. There is no definitive way to tell if our ancestors were more contented than we are today. And yet there *has* been a fierce debate about whether life was better in that long stretch of prehistory.

The key moment in *Homo sapiens'* story was the agricultural (or Neolithic) revolution, which began about 12,000 years ago. As humans learned to cultivate crops and domesticate animals such as cows and pigs, hunter-gatherers started laying down their spears. Instead of moving around to hunt and forage, farmers could make more than enough to eat by staying put and growing wheat, barley, maize and rice.

Needing somewhere to store all this food, villages were settled, then towns, then cities. By 6000 BCE the world's first city – Çatalhüyük in what is now Turkey – was home to around six thousand souls. This maze of mud-brick buildings looks like a honeycomb from above: no streets, just holes in each ceiling through which the Çatalhüyükians could climb, via timber ladders, back down into their home.

In such places there was no need for everyone to farm. Those tending the fields or minding the animals could produce more than enough food to go around, so others were freed to learn new skills: butchery, garment-making, woodwork, politics, religion. They could invent, experiment, collaborate. The birth of cities meant the unfurling of that lofty thing we call 'civilisation'. The rest is (literally) history.

And so the agricultural revolution is the big bang, the giant leap, the definitive before-and-after moment in *Homo sapiens'* rise to world dominance. If population growth equals success, you could argue that this revolution was a great thing for our species as a whole; but were *individuals'* lives better before or after it?

The 17th-century philosopher Thomas Hobbes famously argued that life before agriculture was 'solitary, poor, nasty, brutish and short'.[1] The 'poor' bit is hard to dispute from the vantage point of modern comfort. We pampered creatures start turning up the thermostat in September to stave off the cold – imagine living a lifetime of winters in it. 'Short' is hard to argue with either, with average life spans significantly shorter than we enjoy today.

Yet against the 'nasty and brutish' brigade – who argue that mankind has been on a steady upwards trajectory since 10,000 BCE – there's a rival camp that thinks the total opposite. Renowned historian Jared Diamond has called the agricultural revolution 'the worst mistake in the history of the human race ... a catastrophe from which we have never recovered'.[2]

But why, when farming seeded more food and more freedom? Because it also seeded the concept of property, which seeded hierarchies, which seeded greed, which seeded rivalry, which seeded war, which seeded slavery. Furthermore, although farmers could conjure up a lot more food than foragers, their diet was actually worse and less varied, evidenced by the inches that fell off the average human's height after the agricultural revolution. Disease became rife, too; living cheek by jowl in cities such as Çatalhüyük, tuberculosis and leprosy swept through populations.

Who is right? Was the pre-agricultural world an Eden or a purgatory? Was life for individuals better or worse than what came after?

It is, of course, impossible to chuck the vast spectrum of human experience under the headings 'better' or 'worse'. If you were a wealthy Babylonian merchant in 1700 BCE, life was probably more enjoyable than it was for an ancient hunter-gatherer living through a drought. If you were a mill worker putting in fourteen-hour days in Victorian Britain, life was probably worse than it was for an early human living on the African savannah, who foraged for a few hours before feasting on their bounty, spending time with family and sleeping.

It is naive to paint the pre-agricultural world as a lost Eden. Yet you will know – from the title and thrust of this book – that I believe there were aspects of hunter-gatherer life that *were* more conducive to living contentedly.

Let's switch tenses now, from past to present: there *are* elements of hunter-gatherer life that *are* more conducive to living contentedly. Not all hunter-gatherers laid down their spears during the Neolithic revolution. Thousands of them live today, custodians of a way of life that stretches back two million years.

How hunter-gatherers live now

In the Eyasi Valley of Northern Tanzania, the Hadza still set out to hunt for antelope or birds. On the banks of Brazil's Maici river live the Pirahã, who gather fruits, nuts and small game from the jungle and eat food as they acquire it. On the frozen ice of the Arctic, Inuit still base a large part of their diet on the seal and caribou they have hunted for five thousand years.

Some of the remaining hunter-gatherers have fiercely resisted contact with the outside world, most notably the Sentinelese islanders, who live in the Bay of Bengal. In the 1970s a *National Geographic* film crew came to shore to catch a glimpse of this reclusive tribe, leaving gifts including a live pig and a doll. The Sentinelese killed the pig, buried the doll and shot an arrow into the documentary maker's thigh.[3] They have not been troubled much since.

Other tribes have been friendlier, opening up their homes and lives to the anthropologists and linguists who have turned up to see them over the past century or so. Unlike the hunter-gatherers of prehistory, whose feelings we will never know, these people can talk, share, let us know how they find their life. The results are thought-provoking. Time and again surveys and anthropological reports from these societies find a level of contentment that we in the 'WEIRD' world (Western, educated, industrialised, rich and democratic) can only envy.

Studies have shown that remote Inuit and Maasai tribes have high levels of life satisfaction;[4] that the Himba – remote herding people of North-West Namibia – are significantly more satisfied with life than the urban Himba who have migrated to towns;[5] and that the introduction of market goods and material wealth among the Tsimané people of the Bolivian Amazon has not correlated with increased wellbeing.[6]

Most interesting are the studies of the Hadza people of

Tanzania, one of the last exclusive hunter-gatherer societies on earth. Every morning when the camp wakes there are no stores of food, no grazing animals to slaughter or crops to harvest. Every day they walk out with only sharpened sticks, axes, bows, arrows (and their own wits) to see what they can find.

In the rainy season they might dig up some tubers. In the sun they might chance upon a bush groaning with berries, some tangy baobab fruit or a golden honeycomb lodged in a tree, which they will eat, larvae and all. If they're lucky, the arrow might find a warthog or antelope to feast on.

They live nomadically, setting up camps made of branches and dried grass, moving on when there's more food to be had elsewhere. The Hadza have the oldest mitochondrial DNA ever tested in a human population; scientists reckon that they have been in the same area of Tanzania for at least 50,000 years.

Although there can be no perfect proximation of the lives of ancient hunter-gatherers in the 2020s, the lives of the Hadza are as close as we will get. And are they contented, relative to the rest of us? The answer is a resounding yes.

A study that compared life satisfaction levels between the Hadza and a dozen different cultures and nations found that the hunter-gatherers outscored them all. With an average happiness score of 5.83 on a 7-point scale, they were more contented than those surveyed in Malaysia, Turkey, Italy, Slovakia, the Philippines, Chile, Hong Kong, Spain, Austria, the United States, Mexico – more contented than for every other nation with comparable data.[7]

Many who have observed the world's remaining foragers have

been struck by their contentedness. Daniel Everett, who spent years with the Pirahã in the rainforests of Brazil, marvelled at their freedom from anxiety, depression, panic attacks and suicide.[8] James Suzman, who spent twenty-five years visiting the Ju/'hoansi of the Kalahari, noted their enviable ability to live in the present: 'People never wasted time imagining different futures for themselves or indeed for anybody else.'[9] They work to acquire food for around fifteen hours each week, spending another fifteen to twenty hours on chores. The rest of the time is for relaxation, sleep, and seeing family and friends.

Have you ever dreamed of a life more like this? Does a part of you yearn for simpleness, for stillness, for night skies full of stars? We must be wary of patronising simplifications, of course. The 18th-century ideal of the 'noble savage', uncorrupted by civilised life, now rightfully makes us cringe. Such stereotypes minimise the breadth and depth of these lives. For the Pirahã, the Hadza or any other contemporary foragers, there will still be tragedies and difficult times – and they might well find the idea that they are 'simple people living simple lives' highly irritating.

Nevertheless, as the levels of life satisfaction in 'traditional' societies regularly outdo those in 'WEIRD' societies, and as the comforts of modernity seem to offer such diminishing returns to our own wellbeing, it's worth asking: what do hunter-gatherers get right that we get wrong? What can we learn, both from our foraging ancestors and those alive today? How can we recover elements of the paleolithic life that our instincts tell us are important to us as human beings? Read on to find out.

2

Tribe and Friendship

The coffin is cloaked in white lilies, the crowd in black coats. An organist for hire bashes out 'Abide with Me'. At the end of one pew a mourner stares into the distance, his eyes misting. 'In life, in death, o Lord, abide with me . . .' As the hymn crescendoes, he slumps down, sobs, blows noisily into a tissue, then discreetly checks his notes to remember the name of the guy in the coffin.

Professional grieving has been going on for a long time. Since the days of ancient Egypt, mourners have been hired to wail extravagantly. They even have a name: moirologists. Today, a UK firm offers a 'Rent a Mourner' service, dispatching black-clad actors to the send-offs of strangers where they will be 'sombre' or 'cheery' according to taste. The grief-stricken shell out for this to avoid the shame of a low turnout. But what would be so wrong with that?

While most of us wouldn't think about hiring a moirologist, the fact that such a job exists speaks to a deeply held belief: that popularity is the sign of a successful life. If Uncle Bob's funeral only had three guests, many would view it as a tragedy, even if those were close friends. What matters is the numbers.

In the months leading up to my thirtieth birthday I thought I would break the habit of a lifetime and have a party. Normally, I loathe the spotlight about as much as moths love it, so I had not had a birthday party since Captain Cornflakes was hired to celebrate my sixth. But at the end of a tumultuous decade, something compelled me to put down a deposit on a room above a London pub, with a savoury buffet thrown in.

When the big day was about a month away the panic began to set in. Numbers panic. Who would turn up? The room was big enough to need twenty-five guests without echoing. I could bank on my siblings, my closest girlfriend, my best work friend. But then? Tormented by images of untouched sausage rolls, I toyed with inviting the man who was tiling my bathroom. 'Room meat', they call such people; bodies to fill a space and avoid the shame of low numbers. In the end a jolly time was had by twenty-odd guests but, to be honest, numbers panic ruined it all until I was three Proseccos down.

The obsession with being (and appearing to be) popular is why humble braggers complain of how packed their social calendar is; why Instagrammers show off numerous bunches of birthday flowers; why people clutter the mantelpiece with Christmas cards, a chorus line of Santas proclaiming 'a lot of people like me!' We think, in short, that having many friends and acquaintances means a life well lived. But what if it doesn't?

Why we long for a big tribe

Our desire for popularity is hardwired into us, because for millennia being socially successful meant staying alive. Fifty million years ago our primate ancestors found that by banding together in loose social groups they could better elude the jaws of predators.[1] Those left out in the cold were less likely to make it to the morning. Those who were accepted and received the pack's protection were more likely to pass on their genes. Survival of the fittest meant survival of the friendliest. And so, over the long, dark millennia of prehistory, a desire for social acceptance was hardwired into the primate brain.

By the time early humans evolved about two and a half million years ago, belonging to a tribe was still a matter of life and death. Out on the savannah there was, literally, safety in numbers. Our ancestors kept watch over each other at night, tending fires to warn off predators while others slept. Travelling in groups meant more hands for foraging and hunting. Tribe members shared food, labour and the raising of children. Belonging to a tribe came with a lot of benefits – and pro-social behaviour helped to ensure that you would continue to belong.

To understand how important social acceptance was for hundreds of thousands of years, imagine the sheer terror of being entirely on your own in a predator-filled world. Exclusion from the tribe would have been the signature on the loner's death warrant, which is why we still feel rejection so profoundly hundreds of thousands of years later.

A body of research has found that the pain of being rejected is almost physical. Social psychologists from the University of California had volunteers climb inside an MRI scanner to monitor their brain activity while they played a virtual game of 'Cyberball', in which a ball is thrown between three players. When the virtual players in the game stopped 'throwing' the ball to the volunteer, even this small rejection increased activity in the parts of the brain that respond to physical pain.[2] Another – rather crueller – experiment by Columbia University asked volunteers to look at pictures of ex-boyfriends and -girlfriends who had dumped them. Again, brain scans showed activity in the 'ouch!' parts of the brain.[3]

Sticks and stones may break our bones but being rejected can hurt physically, too. The lonely are more likely to have repeated heart attacks[4] and cancer.[5] Meanwhile, Sally Social enjoys brain-floods of opioid-like chemicals and all sorts of positive physical effects, from an improved heart rate[6] to faster-healing wounds.[7]

How tribes got turbo-charged

Evolution has primed us to seek connection. Most of us are greedy to accumulate contacts, acquaintances and friends, because somewhere deep inside, an ancient voice is crying 'safety in numbers!' For the vast majority of our time on earth, though, that urgent desire to connect was frustrated by geography and circumstance. If you lived in a one-horse town or backwater village, you weren't going to pick up much fresh friendship meat. When you bonded with a stranger over a pint of mead you couldn't swap digits and promise you'd call later. Long after the agricultural revolution, we kept to our tight, intimate tribes.

Then, in the past century, two social revolutions turbo-charged our ability to grow our tribe. The first was telecommunications. Instead of putting pen to paper to keep up with friends, we could pick up the phone. Friendships could be kept alive and arrangements easily made. The telephone dramatically shortened the distance between people, turbo-charging our ability to grow our social networks.

As far as tribe-growing goes, however, the more dramatic revolution came only in the last twenty-five years: social media. This has transformed our tribal possibilities. No longer limited to our friends, neighbours and colleagues, here – at the mere tap of a smartphone screen – are thousands of 'friends' for the taking.

You know what a phone zombie looks like: head bent over their screen, thumb on perma-scroll, unable to look away from their device while walking or cooking or going to the toilet. We have tended to think of these people as 'anti-social' but in fact their instincts are hyper-social. They are obsessively looking for connection.

All those little dopamine hits we get when someone 'likes' our joke on X (formerly Twitter) are echoes from our long-distant past, when being liked meant staying in the tribe and staying alive. This is why the pull of social media is so strong, and why people get lost for hours in an Instagram vortex: by looking at the picture of a distant acquaintance on the beach in Dubai we feel that we are knowing them, and knowing others feeds that ancient hunger for connection.

Of course, where there's a desperate human drive for anything, there's someone making money from it. Social-media companies fast became clever at designing their products in a way that titillates our hyper-social instincts, with algorithms presenting more people and possibilities to connect. If our Stone Age brains are hungry for social connection, they laid on a twenty-four-hour all-you-can-eat buffet, and conceived ways to make those foodstuffs utterly addictive. The result: internet users worldwide now spend around two and a half hours a day on social media.[8]

Meanwhile text messaging and emailing make it easy to keep in touch with a wide circle of 'real-life' friends, acquaintances and colleagues. Whether it's texting the guy we met on a scuba diving course seven years ago, or skimming the latest on the neighbourhood WhatsApp group, we can spend hours maintaining a large social network. The average American now knows around 600 people – and if 'knowing' includes those we might have the odd interaction with online, the true number is a lot higher.[9] Whereas once our tribe size was limited by geography, proximity and culture, now the sky's the limit.

'What's wrong with that?' you might ask. Mae West famously quipped that 'too much of a good thing is wonderful'; surely having too many friends is wonderful, too? Can there really be such a thing as 'too many' relationships with other people, whether online or in real life?

Friendship: quantity vs quality

In the past 12,000 years, since most humans lived as hunter-gatherers, we have made breathtaking scientific progress as a species. We have flown to the moon, split the atom, worked out how to clone living things. But no one has yet worked out how to stretch time. Like our long-distant ancestors, we get a mere twenty-four hours in a day, and in terms of our relationships, this time is now spread far more thinly over a far greater number of interactions.

It is a simple observation that the more friendships we have, the less time and attention we will be able to devote to each – and that, consequently, relationships will suffer. Numerous studies have shown that frequency of contact strengthens ties. One looked at large amounts of data on mobile phone contacts between friends to help explain why some relationships persisted while others 'decayed'. Their finding: 'Stable relationships have and require a constant rhythm . . .' If communication was stop-start, 'most likely the tie will decay'.[10] Research reinforces what we already know: fail to invest enough energy in relationships and they will fizzle out.

For a long time I was haunted by the ghost of Elvis Presley. Specifically, Elvis singing 'You Were Always on My Mind'. It's a love song, but it's also a neglect song – and its notes would haunt me when I realised that I hadn't taken the time to connect with those I loved for ages; 'little things' went unsaid and undone.

The guilt of neglect hummed quietly underneath my busy

existence. When things were less busy, I reasoned, I'd spend more quality time with those I loved. We had a bank of memories to keep us going, didn't we? In the meantime there was just too much to do; too many people to see ...

My mum and I have long enjoyed a June tradition. We watch the Wimbledon ladies' final together, always accompanied by a Caesar salad and a few glasses of Pimm's. As regular as rain on Centre Court, we are sitting in her living room commenting on the grunting of the female players. One Friday a decade or so ago I was looking forward to the annual tennis-fest when I got an email from an American couple I had met overseas months earlier. 'We're in London! Just for the weekend ... Want to meet for lunch tomorrow?' Ah. Tomorrow was Ladies' Final. The journey to my mother's took a couple of hours. Something had to give.

I made the call to mum, who responded as I knew she would: 'It's absolutely *fine*, darling! You *must* go!' So I met these nice people for a few hours on London's South Bank, drinking bottles of beer and talking about whether they should hit Sicily or Majorca next. And on the bus on the way home I thought of how crazy it was to prioritise those I would never see again over the person I adored beyond words. My eyes misted as Elvis crooned in my ear, reminding me that I never took the time ...

Still, I was a repeat offender. Although I knew the people I'd want around me in my dying moments, I didn't grant them many of my living ones. These I spent in the company of colleagues or dates, or attending social functions that I knew I wouldn't really enjoy but felt obliged to go to anyway. I spent a lot of time online, too. The celebrities on Perez Hilton.com and pseuds on Twitter became more vivid and compelling than the people I deeply cared about. One day, I vowed, I'll spend quality time with them. One day. It's just so busy right now! *Scrolls through Facebook*.

We all know, deep down, that digital relationships come a very poor second to face-to-face ones. We have come to think of X and Instagram as replacements to the old hearth around which we would gather to talk about the day, but this is an illusion. Perhaps indulging in these online relationships wouldn't matter so much if our time were infinite, but it's not. We have only twenty-four hours in a day. By devoting so much time to vague acquaintances and strangers online we can't nourish the relationships that matter.

THE PALEO PRESCRIPTION
Choose and cherish your tribe

'You can't choose your family', goes the old saying – but you can choose your tribe. You can consciously weigh the importance of each person you know, from close friends to distant acquaintances, thinking carefully about the space and time they should occupy in your life. The goal: to experience the levels of intimacy and comradeship enjoyed by our ancestors, and by hunter-gatherers today. How can we nourish that ancient part of us which longs for close kith and kin?

Around a decade ago, I started thinking more carefully about how – and to whom – I should apportion my time. It started with a process I call 'social mapping'. This is a way of consciously organising friends, family and acquaintances into different groups according to how well we know them, how they enrich our lives and how much we should invest in them. This might sound rather cold but it is something that human beings have long done, albeit unconsciously.

In the 1990s, evolutionary biologist Professor Robin Dunbar published his groundbreaking 'social brain hypothesis'.[11] This proposed that (because managing relationships takes cognitive effort) the number of meaningful social contacts that we primates can have is limited by the size of our neocortex. For humans, Dunbar argued, that number is around 150.

Throughout human history, groups of around 150 people appear with fascinating regularity, from tribal societies to medieval English villages to modern army units. More interesting to me, though, is Dunbar's argument that 150 is just one of the group sizes that recurs throughout the human story.[12]

Imagine six concentric circles with a person at their centre. The innermost and most intimate circle is a core group of around five people, perhaps the individual's immediate family, spouse or best friend. Next out is a circle of roughly fifteen close family members and really good friends; then a network of fifty more distantly connected family and friends; then a group of the aforementioned 150 people whom the individual can know in a meaningful way. Beyond this are two much bigger circles: 500-odd acquaintances and 1500 people they recognise but don't have much contact with.

While of course these numbers will not be exactly replicated across billions of lives, what is important and striking is the existence of distinct social layers which increase in size as they decrease in intimacy. This unconscious categorisation suggests that we humans – and our primate cousins – have long understood some important truths:

- There are cognitive limits to the number of relationships we can manage
- We can only be truly close to a small number of people
- Our social energy is finite and should be expended thoughtfully

Drawing a social map

Inspired by our innate categorising instincts, social mapping is about clarifying which relationships are the most important, and therefore the priority for our limited time and energy. Though Dunbar's 'social brain hypothesis' suggests six network sizes, for the sake of clarity my own social map contains just three: an innermost circle of **VIPs** (three to five very close family or friends); a **tribe** (around fifteen people who are important to me) and a **wider community** (100–150 more distant friends, relatives, acquaintances and colleagues).

My first round of social mapping started with a mental trawl through everyone I knew, to work out which of these groups they would sit in. And I mean *everyone*: all the names on my phone, old Facebook friends, contacts on LinkedIn, distant relatives in my address book, neighbours I saw every now and again.

With each person, I held their image in my mind and assessed which social network they naturally sat in. Did they belong in my VIPs, my tribe or my wider community? If they didn't fall into any of these, I wouldn't include them on my social map. My contacts spring-clean showed up the guy who fixed computers in my office eighteen years ago, several one-time-only dates I'd met on dating apps, and two people who were actually dead.

If you decide to draw a social map, you might instinctively know where each person goes. For those who are unsure, here are a few pointers as to who might sit where:

VIPs This person is one of the emotional pillars of your life. They know you intimately: your likes and dislikes, hopes and fears. They've probably seen you cry, and vice versa. They know about your childhood, the good bits and bad. You can be candid if they upset you. You care deeply about their wellbeing. If you had to spend a month on a desert island with one other person, they'd be one of the first you'd think of.

Tribe Not a VIP but a good friend or close family member nonetheless. You'd be comfortable calling them by a nickname. You know with reasonable accuracy how they've spent life so far: what they have studied, where they have lived, who they have loved. If you were offered a weekend in a hotel with nothing to do but eat, swim and flop, you could happily spend it with just this person.

Wider community A more distant friend, relative or neighbour. If you bumped into them in a coffee shop, you'd naturally have a catch-up. If they were going through a major life event – getting married, having children, suffering a serious illness – you would know about it and would probably contact them to congratulate or commiserate. At the less familiar fringes of the wider community are acquaintances whom you would cross the street to say 'hi' to.

Once you've sorted your nearest, dearest and most distant into different categories, it's time for a stock-take. How many people are in each of your groups?

Here's a reminder of the numbers I aim for, based loosely on the network sizes that recur throughout the human story:

VIPs three to five people
Tribe around fifteen people
Wider community 100 to 150 people
If you're thinking: *Help! I don't have anything like that many friends/family/acquaintances*, don't fret, smaller numbers mean more of your time and attention to be shared among those who matter most.

If your social mapping has gone the other way, however – revealing large numbers of people appearing in your VIP group or tribe – consider moving some of these people into a less intimate grouping. This might sound brutal, but remember that the end goal is to enrich your most important relationships. There are only so many hours in a day, and only so much social energy we have to expend.

This doesn't mean closing ourselves off to new friendships – clicking with someone is one of life's joys. But it does mean being conscious of our cognitive limits, recognising the basic truth that if we want to improve the quality of our relationships, it's essential to think about the *quantity* of relationships in our lives, too.

Reallocating your time

Once you have a social map – your different social networks sorted according to intimacy – you can use it to allocate your time more consciously. All this might seem rather engineered for the realm of human relationships, which we imagine should flourish effortlessly and organically. But just as long-term romantic partners (particularly those with children) often schedule date nights in order to maintain their connection – knowing that life's demands can relegate relationships to the bottom of the pile – it's wise to counteract the demands of our busy age with some concrete ideas about how often we should be connecting with those we care about the most.

In order to allocate my social resources more mindfully, I've found it helpful to quantify them, with planned interactions falling broadly into one of these three categories:

Contacts are brief, fleeting and low-effort: a text message, a five-minute phone call, a short, chatty email. These interactions don't demand much time or attention; this might simply be messaging someone while watching TV.

Connections are, as the word suggests, a chance to engage in a more meaningful way: meeting for a coffee or lunch, having a chat over a glass of wine, an hour-long phone call. These encounters are about being fully engaged with the other person, hearing what they've been doing and how they are beyond 'I'm fine, thanks!' superficial conversation.

Super-connections are longer occasions that require more effort: a day trip where you've got hours to catch up in the car, a big dinner out, a long country walk, a night away. You're spending hours in someone's company, one to one (or with children, too). You spend enough time together that there are silences as well as conversations. Unlike a brief coffee or phone call, you'll remember the occasion six months later: the time we had gin and tonics on the train on the way to the races, the time we walked all the way along the river together, the night we slept out under the stars.

While quantifying socialising like this might seem odd, I've found this a helpful way of ensuring that my social resources are spread in the way that I want them to be, and that I am truly nurturing my closest relationships rather than letting them wither on the vine while I devote time to those I don't care much about anyway, or scroll through my phone.

If you want to give it a try, you might know, instinctively, how you want to reallocate your time. But if you're looking for a guide, here are the kind of connections I aim for:

VIPs

At least one *contact* a day
At least one *connection* a week
At least one *super-connection* a month

Tribe

At least one *contact* a week
At least one *connection* a month
At least one *super-connection* a year

Wider community

At least one *connection* a year (or one *contact*, for more distant acquaintances)

The balance here might seem surprising. By following the guide above, social time and energy is dramatically shifted towards a small number of people, leaving little for more distant acquaintances.

For me, that's the whole point of this process: narrowing the number of people I really focus on to make sure these relationships are more intimate and rewarding. Living the Paleo Life is about restoring the deep connections that as humans we are designed to have. If modern social habits have been like binge-ing on junky snacks, this is the equivalent of having three good meals a day.

Of course, I don't stick to this religiously. A month or two might go by when I haven't had a 'super-connection' with anybody; when you're with a newborn baby 24/7 it's difficult enough to shower let alone think about scheduling in a deep 'n' meaningful. But the mere fact that I have these ambitions keeps me mindful about how I'm allocating my time. Even vaguely keeping track of my connections and super-connections keeps me accountable. There's no pretending that I've been investing in friendships when I've actually been investing in social media.

If you're trying out social mapping, remember that this is a guide, not a strict set of rules that you have to follow to the letter. If someone you care about in your tribe is demanding more of your time, or if an acquaintance offers you an amazing experience for a day or two, go for it. If dialling down the time you spend on a less-important friendship would cause hurt, don't do it. Trust your gut. What matters most is that you're consistent about devoting time to the central figures in your life, particularly to your VIPs.

Cutting down on faux-cialising

Alongside this reallocation of time among 'real-life' friends, family and acquaintances, I have found it essential to address online socialising – or 'faux-cialising'. Because although it might feel good to banter with strangers on X and leave comments under some distant acquaintance's snaps on Instagram, it isn't real socialising.

These sites keep you hooked with endless scrolling, with notifications and bright shiny colours and the promise – utterly seductive to our Stone Age brains – of thousands of people in the palm of our hand. But it's not nourishing the part of our soul that needs real, touching-distance relationships. Worse, it's distracting from them, leaving less time for them, and even making them look difficult, dull or messy by comparison.

That's why, for me, pushing back against social media and other technological distractions have been a critical part of living the Paleo Life. It's not realistic for most of us to unplug ourselves from the internet completely, but it is important for us to be more mindful about how much time we are spending faux-cialising.

This is far from an easy task. Social-media platforms such as TikTok and Instagram have the same effect on our neural circuitry as gambling and recreational drugs. X users whose messages get reposted or liked experience the same kind of chemical reaction delivered by drugs such as cocaine.

In the next chapter we will look in detail at ways of containing social media, emails and texting so that these technologies don't sprawl across our lives but are contained very carefully within it. The goal of the Paleo Life is not to turn our backs on technology, but to ensure that it is enhancing our lives, not consuming them.

Stone Age wisdom on . . . friendship

- For the vast majority of our existence on earth, we lived in close-knit tribes, seeding in us a craving for social intimacy.
- Achieving this intimacy means rejecting the modern idea that life is a popularity contest, and instead concentrating social effort where it matters.
- Try drawing a 'social map' to categorise all the people in your life into distinct social networks, from your VIPs to distant acquaintances.
- Once you've clarified who matters most, you can consciously reallocate your time towards them.
- Cut down on the online faux-cialising; it wastes valuable time that could otherwise be spent developing richer, real-life relationships.

3

Hierarchy and Status

On the eastern shore of the Hudson in upstate New York stands a vast Gothic ruin: gaping windows, crumbling turrets, fern-covered floors. Almost two centuries ago this was a place of legend. Built for socialite Elizabeth Schermerhorn Jones, of prominent New York family, the Joneses, Wyndcliffe had twenty-three rooms, a boathouse and a three-storey atrium topped with coloured glass. Goaded by this grandeur, other wealthy families competed to build even bigger mansions along the Hudson Valley. The Astors had 2,800-acre Ferncliff, the Vanderbilts a fifty-four-room mega-mansion. The race coined a phrase: 'keeping up with the Joneses'.

It didn't matter that these elites already owned half the Upper East Side; if other millionaires now had turreted fantasies upstate, they would darn well have one too. The same impulse compels us to buy the designer handbag or the house in the best post-code. The same urge drives all those with unimaginable wealth and power to keep on finding ways to beat their rivals; think

Jeff Bezos building the world's tallest yacht, or Donald Trump trying to claim that his inauguration crowd was bigger than Barack Obama's.

Striving to match or outdo our peers is the current that pulls under the surface of our lives, luring us to the shopping mall or the plastic surgeon, keeping us at our desks late at night and propelling us to the gym early in the morning. On a species level, one-upmanship can be a good thing, as it drives human beings to aim higher – sometimes literally. That Neil Armstrong took his small step on the moon in 1969 is partly because the USSR had sent Yuri Gagarin into space in 1961, prompting an envious JFK to vow that the United States would go one better by the end of the decade.

Yet, while comparing and despairing might spur nations to greatness, for individuals the result is most often misery. A stack of studies has found that our wellbeing is based not only on the objective truth about our own success, careers, wealth, health, looks and relationships, but also on how we believe we compare on all these fronts to our peers.[1]

Many years ago I landed the job of chief speechwriter to the prime minister at 10 Downing Street. Sashaying along its thickly carpeted corridors I felt like a *West Wing* character. I liked the status and loved the pay: a £10,000 improvement on my previous salary. Life was good, until some well-intentioned civil servants decided, in the interests of transparency, that all Downing Street advisers' salaries must be made public. As soon as the spreadsheet was online we crowded around a colleague's computer, giddy to find out where we sat in the pecking order. But ... what? What was this? I was on £15,000 less than *her*? £30,000 less than *him*? Seeing those I thought of as direct peers on salaries significantly higher than mine was a punch to the gut. Ignorance had been bliss; knowledge was agony. I would lie awake at 3am burning with resentment. The Joneses had left me in the dust.

Envy's deep roots

Comparison might be the thief of joy, but we are hardwired to indulge in it. The evolutionary roots for envy – and its bedfellow inadequacy – make perfect sense. To pass on our genes we need to attract a mate. To snare one of these we are in competition with others of our own biological sex. To help edge ahead of that pack, it helps to size up the competition, to become aware of our own relative deficits and improve on them. Envy is an alert system, letting us know where we are lacking relative to our peers in order that we can improve our chances of reproducing.

And so, rather cruelly, the human brain evolved to encourage comparing and despairing. Envy stimulates the brain's anterior cingulate cortex, which is associated with both physical and mental pain.[2] Like a cowboy's spur stabbing into the side of a horse to make it run faster, this pain makes us work harder on our looks, careers and wealth generation. Then, when we imagine ways in which we might edge ahead of our rivals – by buying that £200 jacket, say – our brain is flooded with the feel-good neurotransmitter dopamine. Even before we have consciously weighed up whether we can afford the jacket, Mother Nature is whispering: *Buy it! It's going to give you the edge!*

Here's the good news: a propensity to compare and despair is not some defect. It's what human beings are designed to do. We are designed to seek out information about those around us, to see how we compare and, sometimes, to feel the grip of the green-eyed monster. The bad news? Modern life has taken these natural instincts and turned them into instruments of psychological torture.

The Race

Around 12,000 years ago, a guy stood in a field and had an idea. If he could grow enough wheat to have a surplus, he could use this surplus to 'pay' someone else to do the grunt work. So began the long and sorry tale of hierarchy: haves and have nots, kings and peasants, rulers and ruled. So began a pecking order arranged according to money, land, power and influence. So began the great competition between human beings to have more, consume more, enjoy more wealth and status: we'll call it The Race.

Human beings took to hierarchy fast. The Sumerians (4100–1750 BCE) had a ruling class, an upper class, middle class, working class and enslaved class. In ancient Egypt (3100–332 BCE) a pyramid topped by the pharaoh had the vizier, nobles, priests, scribes, soldiers, craftsmen, farmers and slaves below him. In ancient Rome (753 BCE–476 CE) plebeians couldn't marry patricians, no matter how much money they had.

At least those born into strictly hierarchical societies could console themselves that their relative misfortune wasn't their 'fault'. If there's zero social mobility, you can hardly beat yourself up for failing to get far in The Race. A more acute emotional pain has come for those living in rampantly unequal societies where there is at least the promise of meritocracy. If you grow up hearing rags-to-riches stories, but you're still in rags, what does that say about you? Loser.

As The Race speeded up, humans designed an elaborate series of medals to show who was winning. In ancient Phoenicia, you wore the colour purple to show that you could afford the expensive dye, made by sea snails. In the Middle Ages you wore crackowes, long pointy shoes so ridiculous that Edward III had to ban those that were over a certain length. In Tudor times aristocrats were proud to display blackened teeth, as it showed that you could afford to eat sugar. In the 17th century you displayed a real pineapple in your home to show you were Mr Big (worth about £5,000 in today's money).

We might pity those silly folk from the past but swap purple rags for Prada bags and coal-black teeth for bright white veneers and it's clear that while the symbols of wealth might change, the yearning to show how far ahead in The Race we are doesn't. 'Check out my pineapple! Look at my ridiculously long shoes, my Steinway in the hall, my gold wallpaper, my Rolex Daytona ...' As the vast juggernaut of global capitalism chuntered into action, The Race to consume ever more conspicuously speeded up: *How can they afford a BMW? So she's wearing Louboutins now?*

For the past century a stylishly bespectacled crowd has

been cheering on The Race and urging us to run faster, faster. Advertising executives in Soho or on Fifth Avenue might not see themselves as architects of insecurity, but this trillion-dollar business is built on a simple formula: compare, despair, buy. Pssssst, watch this ideal woman with her ideal body live an ideal life. Now let your mind drift to your own lumpen body, your dull days, bland home, flat relationship. Feeling inadequate? Simple: buy this lovely new thing/thong/cream/car/holiday to close the gap! For a hundred years we have been bombarded with images of beautiful, happy people living ideal lives, not only in advertising but in films, TV shows and glossy magazines.

The Race goes supersonic

Throughout the 20th century The Race speeded up. Then, on 4 February 2004, it went supersonic. On that night Mark Zuckerberg set up an online network for his fellow Harvard students, and the world shifted on its axis. Today, Facebook has over three billion active users, getting on for half the planet. They are drawn to the site like flies to honey not only because it allows them to connect but also because it allows them to compare themselves to others in The Race.

Remember the evolutionary roots of comparing? This is not just something we do to pass the time; at a deep, deep level we human beings believe that comparing ourselves to others is essential to our survival, and to our chances of reproducing.

Our ancient brain tells us that if we compare ourselves to other people, their looks, lives, jobs and mates, the more information we will have to jostle up the pecking order. 'Know your rivals ...' whispers the old brain. 'Keep up with the competition!'

This was reasonable advice when you lived in a tribe of thirty others. When you 'live' in a virtual community of 3 billion others, it is a disaster. Who can compete with countless strangers curating their lives to look as glamorous and happy as possible? Whose real existence will measure up well against a show-reel of artfully edited lives?

Over 12,000 years, The Race has established itself in our societies and minds as the way that human beings must live. From our earliest years we learn about hierarchy and status. From our teenage years we compare and despair, looking disconsolately on our own bodies and lives. From our twenties we rush to buy the best things, houses and cars we can afford, because these are things that people of a certain status and station have. And always, always, humming along behind all that is the knowledge that we are in a great race against other human beings.

Some would argue that The Race is just an inescapable part of belonging to the human race; they think that endless competing, desiring and dissatisfaction are inevitable. We are always going to compare ourselves and want what we don't have, aren't we? That's just the ugly business of being human, right? Not according to hunter-gatherers, it isn't.

A life free from hierarchy, comparing and despairing

Although modern life loves to torture us with endless invitations to compare, despair and want, hunter-gatherer life tends to be remarkably free of hierarchy, status and their related discontents. Over the past few centuries, explorers and anthropologists have observed dozens of foraging societies and found a clear thread running through them: egalitarianism. Before the agricultural revolution there were no big chiefs bossing everyone around, no aristocrat class, no peasants. Food was shared out fairly, no matter who hunted it.

For hunter-gatherers, living as equals isn't some nice fluffy way of ordering society – it is essential to survival. Imagine you've stalked through the bush for hours and come home without so much as a rotten fig. You rely completely on the willingness of others to share their riches from the day's hunt and forage. Tomorrow, if they've had a bad day, they might rely on you. Given the unpredictability of hunting and foraging, sharing and cooperation are essential – and one-upmanship or competitiveness a recipe for gradual extinction.

There's no 'I' in team, and there can be no big 'I am' in a hunter-gatherer tribe. Guarding against self-aggrandisement is, therefore, something they take extremely seriously. In the late 1960s the American anthropologist Richard B. Lee lived for years among the !Kung bushmen of the Kalahari. One Christmas he decided to treat his friends to a festive feast, picking out the biggest and meatiest ox he could find at the local market. Alas, this wasn't well received. The bushmen started pulling him aside to tell him how lousy the ox looked: a 'bag of bones', 'a scrawny thing', 'What did you expect us to eat off it, the horns?'[3]

Confused by these attacks – for the animal was clearly a feast-in-waiting – Lee asked an elder what was going on. The response: 'When a young man kills much meat, he comes to think of himself as a big man, and he thinks of the rest of us as his inferiors. We can't accept this ... So we always speak of his meat as worthless. In this way, we cool his heart and make him gentle.'

Lee had been the victim of a long-held ritual known as 'insulting the meat', a way of taking the mighty down a peg or two – or not letting them get mighty in the first place. Cultural anthropologists call this a 'levelling mechanism', and in these societies it works well to deter boasting, arrogance and other behaviours that might poison the harmony of a tight-knit tribe.

Levelling mechanisms guard against anyone getting too big for their boots – and so too does the hunter-gatherers' lack of material possessions.

For a long time the view was that hunter-gatherers' lives were marked by deprivation. Then, in 1966, economist Marshall Sahlins put forward a dramatically different idea, describing hunter-gatherers as 'the original affluent society'.[4] Given their lack of food-stuffed refrigerators and fancy cars, that might seem a strange description, but Sahlins was making the point that affluence is defined by access to the things we desire – and the hunter-gatherers he studied had all they desired.

Although they didn't have much, they didn't *want* much.

They were not tortured by unattainable dreams. They had managed to escape the endless yearning for more. As anthropologist James Suzman (who spent years living among the Ju/'hoansi of the Kalahari) observes, 'they had mastered the art of not obsessing about whether the grass was greener on the other side'.[5]

Although we cannot rewind the clock 20,000 years, it seems reasonable to assume that our prehistoric ancestors were similarly untroubled by thoughts of greener grass on the other side. Sure, men may have looked resentfully at another hunter's pile of animal skins. Women may have envied the beauty of the clan. But their lives offered limited opportunity to compare and despair. When you lived in a tribe of only thirty to fifty others, your pool of competitors was small. When there were no status symbols, you wouldn't feel inadequate about what you didn't have. When you didn't know how people were living in the next valley, you couldn't envy their lives. When there was no grand pecking order, you couldn't feel bad about all those above you. They were free, in short, of The Race.

THE PALEO PRESCRIPTION
Opt out of The Race

Counter-culture folk used to talk about 'sticking it to The Man', The Man being the government or some other authority that oppresses people and grinds them down. The rest of this chapter is about sticking it to The Race: The Race being the great competition to have more, do more, be more wealthy and more successful than others.

We can't flatten inequalities, overturn the class system or bring global capitalism to its knees, but we *can* work to tune out the messages that slot us above or below other human beings, and that attack our self-worth and wellbeing. Imagine that The Race is a real running race being blared out of a television screen, along with a deafeningly loud commentary about who is ahead or behind – and how you're doing. We're not aiming to stop the race from being run (impossible), but we can turn down the commentary that keeps banging on about it (achievable).

Turning down the commentary started for me by identifying my 'envy triggers': those things, people and moments that tended to send a stinging arrow of envy or inadequacy to my heart. There is a Zen saying that 'A flower does not think of competing with the flower next to it. It just blooms.' I will never be that flower. Some of us are especially disposed to envy – and alas I am one of them. Since I was a girl, my green-eyed monster has had fangs and claws.

In 1986, my five-year-old self watched another girl called Claire on *Top of the Pops* singing her hit single, entitled 'It's 'orrible being in love (when you're eight and a half)'. Only three years older than me and a pop star: the jealousy! As a teenager I would woefully compare myself to the other girls in PE class: their already sizeable busts straining at grown-up bras while my non-assets were safely contained in an M&S vest. As a twenty-something I would pore over interviews with successful people my age feeling tortured by the knowledge that I had not done anything half so notable.

By my mid-thirties I was both exhausted by envy and increasingly aware that this was because my poor old Stone Age brain was being goaded by levels of comparison it couldn't cope with. I vowed to scan my life for envy triggers and, where possible, eliminate them. The list was long. It included watching *Keeping Up With the Kardashians*, reading interviews with high-flying career women, catching up with a colleague who was always falling over herself to talk about her super-sociable life, even walking around some of the most beautiful parts of London, with shuttered mews houses that I would never own. But the biggest trigger of all? The engine of envy: social media.

Turn off the envy engine

We have long known that others enjoyed glamorous lives, grand homes and lovely holidays. The trouble these days is the *intricacy* of this knowledge. We know that their spouse celebrated Valentine's Day with a quirky treasure hunt around their house, while ours cursorily signed their name in a garage-bought card. We know that other parents used lockdown as a chance to build forts out of sofa cushions while we turned on *Paw Patrol* for hours. We know that they are having an Aperol spritz overlooking the Grand Canal while we are filling in our tax return.

We might say to ourselves that this is just the 'highlight reel' of other lives. We might reason that they have bad days too, that they have to do the laundry, get caught in the rain, shout at their children from time to time. But however much we think we can rationalise that glorious parade of images on Instagram, it is shaping the way we perceive others' lives and casting an unflattering light on our own. Each post we look at knocks us a little bit further down our imaginary pecking order. For our Stone Age brains – hardwired to compare and envy – this is poison.

I used to be a voracious consumer of other people's lives on social media. By my mid-thirties the comparing-and-despairing largely focused on those getting married and having babies, things I dearly wanted to do myself. Social media opened windows into lives of happy chaos, where two year-olds frolicked in tutus, and Sunday roasts at home featured a cast of thousands of friends. My internal camera would then pan out to my own existence in a small one-bed flat, where I hadn't entertained a guest for months, and where the local curry house knew without asking that I wanted the chicken biryani. I felt as small as an ant.

In all the actions I describe in this book, cutting out social media is perhaps the most important. Doing that began with a recognition of the damage it was doing to me. I had to recognise that although this felt like a diversion I loved in the moment – because Mother Nature was prodding me to compare myself to others – this was corroding my self-esteem. For me, consuming a show reel of beautiful lives was the mental equivalent of downing a pint of hydrochloric acid. It had to stop.

Conduct a social-media audit

- For a couple of weeks, do some research on how you feel after consuming your usual diet of social media.
- For each site you visit regularly, ask yourself how you feel after you've been looking at it: inspired and diverted – or envious and inadequate?
- Are these sites enriching your life in a way that makes them worth the time and any negative feelings they might create?
- After scrolling, are you aware of wanting more: more clothes, more money, more holidays, more success, more recognition, more followers?
- Once you've identified the social-media sites – or individual accounts – which tend to trigger negative feelings, start thinking about how to reduce their presence in your life.

Break the smartphone stranglehold

There are many helpful things you can do to decrease the pull of social media. You can go to the settings function on your phone and turn off notifications. If you've identified particular accounts whose main goal is to inspire envy, you can delete them. You can download apps like AppBlock or

Freedom, which allow you to block social media for certain periods of time.

I did all these things, but still heard the siren song of the smartphone in my pocket. I would find myself reaching for my phone for anything – checking the time, seeing when the rain might stop . . . Before long, I would be gazing at images or reading posts which turned up the commentary on The Race again. It was too easy to let my guard down. The lure of the internet – and the unhelpful messages it can transmit – was so strong that I had to go further.

Most of us know the fierce and addictive grip that smartphones can have on our waking lives. I know people who will not go to the toilet without theirs. A third of teenagers take their smartphone to bed, a digital update on the teddy bear. Many people are so desperate to distance themselves from their devices that they pay thousands for digital detox retreats; on one of them there's even the option to disconnect your room from the internet thanks to signal-blocking paint (just £440 a night).

My solution to smartphone tyranny is simpler and cheaper: an old-fashioned Nokia. Not a smartphone but a dumbphone. If anyone needs me, or if there's an emergency, I have a means of communication. But – blissfully – it comes with no internet to tempt me or envy triggers to taunt me. This is easily the best £35 I have ever spent. I have splashed 100 times this amount on supposedly life-changing holidays, the effects of which lasted less time than my suntan. For £35 I have bought myself freedom from the thing that was dominating my days, stealing my attention and regularly depressing my mood.

In the past decade or so we have developed the ridiculous fear that we won't cope without a smartphone. What if we urgently need something: a map, directions to the nearest pizzeria, the year that Rick Astley made it to number one, to settle an argument? Incredibly, though, not long ago we coped without these instant answers.

I still have my smartphone, because this is the 2020s, and sometimes – such as on holiday – I want to be able to check emails away from home. But day to day, I simply don't need it. And so, day to day, my poor old smartphone goes to jail. Its prison is a combination lock box which cost around £10. There it sits for most of the time.

Like millions of others I used to keep my smartphone on my bedside table to act as my morning alarm. Then, once I'd turned off the alarm, a mysterious invisible glue would mean I found it impossible to put down the phone again – there were sites to scan, news to check ... so now the smartphone is locked up at night, too, replaced by a simple alarm clock.

This doesn't mean I never look at the internet. Instead, I have just wound the clock back to a not-so-distant time – the early noughties – when the internet was a treat to enjoy every now and then rather than a round-the-clock preoccupation. I carefully curate those sites that are going to inspire delight or interest, not envy and inadequacy. To some the idea of imprisoning their smartphone and going back to the days of 'brick' phones will seem extreme or absurd. But given the fierce hold that smartphones have on our attention – and thus our emotions – to me it's a sensible and simple way of regaining control. Cry freedom!

Tune out the wants

Sticking it to The Race, hunter-gatherer style, means getting better at distinguishing what we want from what we really need. In 1928 a leading Wall Street banker named Paul Mazur wrote about how to get the US economy booming. A society, he wrote, 'can be trained to desire change, to want new things even before the old have been entirely consumed ... man's desires can be developed so that they will greatly overshadow his needs'.[6] The following year, US President Herbert Hoover gave a speech to advertising executives in which he enthused, 'You have taken over the job of creating desire and have transformed people into constantly moving happiness machines; machines which have become the key to economic progress.'

You don't have to be a communist to find these words dispiriting. Capitalism requires that we spend, spend, spend. Our desires must be endlessly stoked, our yearning to surge ahead in The Race provoked. And so we constantly moving happiness machines are bombarded daily by images of things and services that will only make us 'happier' still. City dwellers can be exposed to around 3,500 marketing messages in a single day.[7]

What can be the harm? It's just wallpaper, right? But this bombardment brings with it a message that on just the other side of a purchase there's a better life. All this makes us feel inadequate about what we don't have, as suggested by a huge study of more than 900,000 citizens. Researchers compiled life satisfaction data from these people across twenty-seven European countries over thirty years, and compared it with the annual advertising spending in those nations over the same time. The extraordinary finding: one or two years after a notable increase in that country's spend on advertising, there was a measurable dip in life satisfaction levels. So much for constantly moving happiness machines.[8]

Key to sticking it to The Race is opting out of these messages. In Homer's *Odyssey*, Odysseus is warned about the song of the sirens, which will lure his men – and their ship – onto the rocks. He doesn't tell his men to be strong and ignore the song: he instructs them to stop their ears with wax so that they can't hear it. Similarly, it's a good idea to stop our eyes and ears to advertising as far as possible. You can't be influenced if you're not paying attention. You can't want things if you don't know they exist. That's why, for almost a decade, I have tried to remove as much advertising from my life as possible.

Go AWOL from advertising

- Use screening services such as Netflix to avoid television adverts. Record TV programmes so that you can fast-forward through the adverts. If watching in real time, mute and avoid the ad breaks.
- Block pop-up ads on your computer.
- If reading newspapers and magazines, be mindful that

---

up to half the content is advertising; cover the ads as you go.

- Mindless shopping leaves us meandering around environments that are plastered with adverts. Go with a specific purchase in mind, or shop online.
- Unsubscribe from all email newsletters that bombard you with daily deals.
- Put a sign on your door requesting 'no junk mail'.
- In the UK, look online for the Royal Mail opt-out form to ask them to stop delivering brochures to your address; also contact the Direct Marketing Association and ask to opt out of junk mail.
- Unfollow those on social media who frequently promote products or who are selling a lifestyle with products attached.

Master the urge to consume

However much we reduce the influence of advertising or social media in our lives, we have already absorbed so much of the messaging around The Race. We'll still know which the cool brands are, still have that anxious feeling that life will be better if we purchase this Shiny New Product. I have a long history of spending money on pointless stuff. A few years ago I developed an Amazon Prime addiction, which I realised was out of hand when I ordered within minutes a bath pillow, a miniature food processor, three rolls of Hello Kitty stickers and a pressure washer. As soon as I have this stuff in my hands it turns to junk. These days I use the following strategies to combat my urge to consume:

Have a cool-off period before buying

We keep an old-fashioned paper diary on the kitchen counter for family appointments. If I decide I want to buy something on, say, 6 June, I flick through to 6 July and write the potential purchase there. If, a month later, it still seems like a reasonable purchase, I will go ahead and buy it. More often than not, the urge has passed.

Be a satisficer, not a maximiser

Psychologists suggest that there are two main types of decision-makers: 'maximisers' and 'satisficers'. When it comes to what we buy, maximisers will do endless research to find the best version of an item, whereas satisficers pick one that meets their basic needs. I used to be a maximizing consumer, spending hours researching for cars that could drive smoothly at 120 miles an hour, or computers that had huge memories I would never use. Now I deliberately go in the opposite direction, avoiding the lure of the 'top' brand to buy whatever fits my basic requirements. Gaining mastery over the urge to buy the best or the branded is far more satisfying than buying the 'best' product ever was.

Have a no-spend month

Every year, for the whole of October, I spend not a single penny on non-essential items. There is no special significance about October; it just happened to fall around the time I decided on a no-spend month. It also helps the coffers recover a little before the inevitable Christmas splurge. Like the cooling-off period, this no-spend month is remarkably effective at reminding me that what I *want* is very different from what I *need*.

Run the anti-Race

So far in this chapter we've been exploring practical actions to counteract the hierarchy- and status-obsessed society we live in. But sticking it to The Race requires more than this. It needs a change in mindset, too – even a change in the way we see ourselves.

Hunter-gatherers live with fewer wants, less envy, less feeling that the grass is greener on the other side. Much of this, I would argue, must be down to the way they view themselves in relation to others, and the importance they attach to their own lives. Living in egalitarian societies that depend on harmony for their survival, there can be no ego-tripping or domineering. Any narcissistic behaviour is ridiculed ruthlessly – which must, over a lifetime, inculcate a mindset of humility about the individual's place in the scheme of things.

Today, in contrast, narcissism rules. In individualistic societies we have been increasingly encouraged to think of ourselves as highly important people, the centre of our universe. 'You're worth it,' say the advertisers. 'You matter' goes the modern mantra. This might sound empowering but actually it disempowers us by placing pressure on us to be special. It makes us fret endlessly about how we are doing in The Race.

So as far as possible I try to think like the hunter-gatherers: not viewing my own life as unique, but seeing myself as a face in the crowd, an infinitesimally small part of the human story. As the poet Longfellow put it: 'O great Eternity! | Our little life is but a gust | That bends the branches of thy tree, | and trails its blossoms in the dust!'[9] Life is transient, a gust, insignificant. When you re-frame it in this way, the futility of The Race is clarified: does it *really* matter if I'm ahead or behind? Will I *ever* feel that I'm winning? Will surging ahead of the pack bring the rewards it promises? Ninety-nine per cent of the time, the answer is no.

Stone Age wisdom on ... opting out of The Race

- We've been taught since our earliest years that life is a race against others to acquire status, wealth and popularity, and it's making many miserable.
- For most of our time on earth we lived in tribes free of hierarchy and unburdened by materialism.
- Although it's impossible to recreate a lost world, we can take steps to distance ourselves from The Race.

- Tune in to what your 'envy triggers' are – the places, people and experiences that cause you to compare and despair – and try to avoid them.
- Work on breaking away from social media's magnetic pull, even by locking away your technology for chunks of each day.
- Avoid advertising wherever possible, taking steps to remove its insidious messaging from your life.
- Master the urge to consume by delaying purchases, giving you the time to clarify your wants from your needs.
- Change your mindset, resisting the urge to compare and compete by embracing indifference to The Race instead.

4

News and Views

On 18 April 1930 a BBC newscaster sat down in front of the microphone to read the evening bulletin. He cleared his throat and said, simply: 'There is no news.' No wars, plagues, famines, murders, extreme weather events – at least not that they deemed worthy of reporting. For the rest of the fifteen-minute news slot, light piano music was played.

How unthinkable this seems in a time when we can gorge on headlines and exclusives from morning to night. A scan through the morning's papers will take us from an African coup to an Asian drought to a mass shooting in America, all before we have buttered our toast. Many reach for the phone on their bedside table to scroll through the news before they have even got out of bed, as though it were essential to know the latest before a trip to the bathroom.

In 2000, before we could take the news with us on our smartphones, my family took a trip to a remote Greek island. As a voracious consumer of news, I expected to be able to pick up an

English newspaper there. Alas, there were none to be had. Like Robinson Crusoe marooned away from the rest of the world, I wondered endlessly about what was happening back home, despite the fact this was August when nothing much seems to happen at all.

Finally, after a boatload of tourists from another island had descended on the harbour and left again, I found a crinkly two-day-old copy of the *Daily Telegraph* on a café table. So delighted was I with this discovery that it might have been one of the Dead Sea Scrolls. After over two decades I can still remember the picture on the front page: reality TV villain 'Nasty Nick' leaving the Big Brother house. Though the holiday home contained plenty of excellent books to read, I devoured every word of this newspaper three times over.

Why? Why do we hunger for news? Why do we gobble up stories that don't concern us at all, of minor elections in far-flung countries, of the ugly divorce proceedings of wealthy people, of the machinations of obscure politicians? Why do news junkies refresh the home pages of news organisations, hoping for a new angle, or read minute-by-minute updates on live blogs? The answer begins, as ever, millennia ago.

Meet the informavores

For decades, archaeologists have been perplexed by a tiny detail found in many cave paintings: series of dots and other small symbols that appear alongside images of animals. What did they mean? The code was cracked not by experts but by a London furniture conservator called Ben Bacon. Fascinated by these mysterious marks, he spent long hours in the London Library looking at hundreds of pictures of cave paintings.

Finally, he cracked it. The markings related to lunar months, enabling our ancestors to time and track the life cycles of the animals around them.[1] By gathering information, they could start predicting when the animals would migrate or mate or breed. By collecting data they could master their environment, plan for the future and improve their chances of survival.

When we talk of the gathering our ancestors did, we usually mean the gathering of roots, nuts and berries. But the gathering of information was equally important. Each day, members of the tribe had to get enough food to sustain several people. To succeed, you had to constantly seek information: where are the baobab trees groaning with fruit? Where do the wildebeest roam when the days are short? What's that noise in the bushes?

If a hunter-gatherer stuck to the same plains and wasn't interested in exploring further, they would stand a worse chance of surviving and reproducing. Those who were adept at seeking and gathering information were more likely to survive and pass on their genes. We are descended from the curious, the explorers, the need-to-know-morers. As the American psychologist George Miller put it, we humans are 'informavores'. Just as omnivores seek and consume food to survive, informavores seek and consume information to thrive.[2]

So important is the seeking of information to our survival that the human brain evolved to reward the discovery of information in the same way that it rewards the finding of food.[3] As we scroll through news stories our brain is hoping for a feel-good hit of the neurotransmitter dopamine – the bigger the story or scandal, the bigger the hit.

Our ancestral hunger for news

Given the importance of information to our survival – and the fact that finding new information feels good – it's highly likely that our prehistoric ancestors would have been as interested in news as we are. Since language doesn't fossilise we can't know about how news was exchanged between ancient hunter-gatherers, but we do know that in many of the preliterate societies observed over the past few centuries, there was a strong desire for news. Wherever missionaries, anthropologists and other observers travelled, they noted the eagerness of local people to gather fresh information.

L.H Samuelson, a missionary's daughter who lived among the Zulus of South Africa in the 19th century, marvelled at the speed with which oral news could travel. After exchanging brief pleasantries, Zulus meeting on the way to somewhere would ask 'Tell me the news of the country.' This eagerness to know and to share meant that 'whatever takes place is known for miles around, in an incredibly short time … what happens in the morning is known everywhere, long before sunset'. When in 1872 the Zulu king died 300 miles away, Samuelson heard it on the grapevine long before it was published in the settlers' newspapers.[4]

Before these societies had access to the printing press or electricity, they used any means to spread news. The Fox Indians of the Midwest had 'ceremonial runners' who would go on journeys across the territory each spring and autumn to gather news and to spread it. The Zulu king employed messengers to take vital information to regional chiefs. From 19th-century Vietnam to 20th-century Morocco, news criers were observed, proclaiming or singing the day's events to gathered crowds.

Why we've become news junkies

The desire to exchange information has been with us forever. But while we humans have always been keen for news and gossip, in prehistoric times there would have been natural limits on the amount of information we could consume, given that the global population was around 26,000 times smaller.[5] With people spread so thinly, the chance of random conversations by the watering hole (the prehistoric water cooler) would have been slim.

Fast-forward tens of thousands of years to the limitless information on offer in the 21st century, courtesy of the internet. Because our Stone Age brains still perceive the gathering of information as essential to survival, we gorge on it. The ever-changing news cycle offers several opportunities a day for us to have little dopamine highs, as we discover new pieces of information – even if that information is utterly irrelevant to us.

Whereas biology drives our hunger for news, modern culture

encourages it. Being hooked on new information is the 21st century's only acceptable addiction. Addicts to food or drugs or alcohol may be shamed as 'fatties', 'junkies' or 'alkies', but addicts to news are lauded as well-informed citizens, whose knowledge is vital to holding power to account. 'A nation of sheep will beget a government of wolves', as the great American newscaster Edward R. Murrow once said. We have bought into the idea that to guard against tyranny we must arm ourselves with the truth, which in reality means refreshing the news website several times an hour just in case we're a few minutes late to the breaking news party.

Because most of us want to feel like good, admirable people, the implied virtuousness of being abreast of the news makes news-seeking even more addictive. When the alcoholic reaches for another can of super-strength cider, they don't feel that they are doing wider society a favour, but with every scroll of a news website or browse of the latest news post on Facebook, the news addict feels that they are being a virtuous and helpful citizen. Thus news strengthens its grip.

Now for the bad news . . .

If we were hooked on news that was largely positive and life affirming, that might be less of a problem for our wellbeing. But although we moan about the preponderance of bad news, we hunger for it. Studies have shown that given a choice, news consumers will read stories on corruption, scandal, war and terrorism over anything positive.[6] In 2014 a Russian website called the City Reporter decided to report only good news for a whole day. The result? Two-thirds of their readership disappeared.

Our desire for bad news is not because we are sadists who enjoy others' misfortune. It's because of what psychologists call 'negativity bias': human beings' in-built tendency to give more weight to negative experiences than to positive ones. For our ancestors it made sense to focus on the sabre-toothed tiger to your left rather than the beautiful sunset to your right. To survive you had to give more cognitive space to threats and negative experiences than to opportunities and positive experiences. This resulted in a skewed perspective, which persists today. As psychologist Rick Hanson puts it, 'the brain is like Velcro for negative experiences and Teflon for positive ones'.[7]

The negativity bias is why we might disregard twenty compliments and fixate on one minor criticism. It's why we might not book a hotel because, as well as numerous five-star reviews, there was one two-star slating. And it is also why we are more interested in consuming bad news than good news. Our Stone Age brain is programmed to detect concerning information – and where there's a rolling buffet of such information, we will gorge on it.

The news industry knows what generates interest, so it should hardly be surprising that it majors on the bad, sad, frightening and infuriating. For seven years I wrote a weekly newspaper column for *The Times*, covering current affairs. When starting out, I had lunch with a veteran columnist. For the price of some sushi in a Soho restaurant he was to furnish me with some tricks of the trade. After several plates of eye-wateringly expensive sashimi, this respected journalist offered me one pearl of wisdom: 'Make 'em angry, or make 'em anxious. Do that and you've done your job.'

Although this was distasteful advice, in a commercial sense he was bang on. Most of the news is not about faithfully conveying the facts; it's about entertaining and engaging new audiences, viewers and readers. As our attention becomes ever more fragmented and the sources of news multiply, the provocation used to hook us in gets gaudier by the year. *Breaking news! We look inside the murder scene. New details just in . . .*

What this is doing to us

In the 1960s sci-fi novel *Stranger in a Strange Land*, by Robert A. Heinlein, a human who has been raised on Mars returns to earth, seeing the ways of the little green planet through fresh eyes. One thing that strikes the neo-Martian is earthlings' obsession with the news: 'Most neuroses and some psychoses can be traced to the unnecessary and unhealthy habit of daily wallowing in the troubles and sins of five billion strangers.'[8] Today it's over eight billion strangers. What does wallowing in all those 'troubles and sins' do to us?

In April 2013 two bombs ripped through the finish line of the Boston Marathon, killing three people and injuring hundreds. At the time this happened, researchers from the University of California were conducting a study of the mental health of 5,000

Americans. By chance, some of those involved in the study were affected first hand, either by being in the vicinity of the bombing or being connected to someone injured or killed.

Although it was hardly surprising that their mental health suffered in the wake of the tragedy, the researchers were shocked to find that another group were *more* prone to acute stress in the aftermath: those who had consumed more than six hours of news coverage a day in the week following the bombing.[9] Think about that: watching images of the tragedy play out over and over again was in some cases more traumatising than actually being there.

Study after study shows that it's not just *knowledge* of a major news event that impacts us, but the extent to which we've marinated our brains in coverage of the event. Whatever the horror or tragedy – 9/11, the Sichuan earthquake of 2008, the 2014 Ebola crisis or the 2015 terror attacks in Paris – clear links have been found between the amount of news people are exposed to in the wake of these events, and their likelihood of developing anxiety or PTSD.[10]

The news can cause us stress, anxiety, depression. It can spike our levels of cortisol, raise our heart rate, and even increase our chances of having a heart attack years later. My belief is that a lot of this stress is caused by how powerless the news makes us feel. Prehistoric hunter-gatherers were driven to be information-seeking machines because seeking information helped them to find food, evade predators and survive. This was information human beings could use and act upon.

Now we are overloading ourselves with news that – while

important – is useless to us. We can't use it or act on it. I know of many British people who have dedicated countless hours to following news about Donald Trump, causing them significant stress and anger. They feast on every morsel of information about this man, despite the fact that they have no vote in a US election and that it leaves them stewing in rage. By watching news that has nothing to do with us, we are cultivating a sense of powerlessness.

Scroll, scroll, breakdown

For five years I worked as the chief speechwriter in Downing Street. News was the lifeblood of the building, the topic of most conversations. The day in Number 10 was structured around news coverage. At 8am a dozen or so people would gather in the prime minister's office to discuss what was running on the morning bulletins and how we should react. Throughout the day *Sky News* or *BBC News* played in our offices, eyes incessantly drawn to the ticker tape on the bottom of the screen promising *BREAKING NEWS* . . . At 4pm another meeting would take place in the prime minister's office: what were they running with on the six o'clock bulletins? Which ministers were we putting up for the evening broadcasts? How could we make tomorrow's *Daily Mail*?

Modern politics has become a branch of media management, and when you're working in it you simmer in news from morning until night. Having stewed in breaking developments all day, I would finish work around 9pm, come home and slump on my sofa with a glass of Pinot Grigio in one hand and my smartphone in the other, to scroll through the thoughts of the commentariat. Were they being positive about the day's speech? Were there any themes or arguments I could lift for the latest one I was writing? The TV would go on at 10pm for the evening news; before bed I might round off the day's news consumption by reading a few opinion pieces from the various newspapers I subscribed to online.

I knew how much time I was wasting reading news online. I could feel the hours trickling away like dirty water down a drain, yet I couldn't stop. At every opportunity – waiting for the water for my potatoes to boil, even going to the toilet – my thumb would do its familiar dance over my smartphone screen to open up the same news sites or social-media platforms. My excuse (for don't all addicts have excuses?) was that as a political speechwriter I needed my finger on the pulse. Alas, my finger never left it.

Then came the meltdown. We had travelled up to Manchester for the party's annual conference and the prime minister's biggest speech of the year. The long address had taken me weeks to write, with a long and painful drafting process involving a cast of (what felt like) thousands. The whole process ended with me holed up in a hotel room in Manchester for seventy-two hours making frantic last-minute revisions, breathing stale air for days, surrounded by room-service trays of half-eaten burgers.

While thousands schmoozed and partied at the conference outside, I stayed at my laptop in my bunker – my only company the twenty-four-hour TV news. As the countdown to the Big

Speech began, TV reporters would speculate endlessly about what the prime minister was to say. 'He really needs to pull something out of the bag ... His party are expecting big things ...' Although I was not delivering the speech myself, it still felt as though my head was on the block. With each news report the belt of anxiety around my chest would ratchet a notch tighter.

Finally, the morning of the speech. The usual hectic rushing around as I checked the autocue text, briefed the press team on the exclusive extracts we were giving to the media, rushed to the conference hall to skid into my seat. As the lights came up and warm-up music pumped out of the speakers, I looked at all the reporters around me, notebooks at the ready, poised to pull the work of weeks to pieces. As the prime minister took to the stage I felt the lights start to dance, the oxygen leave the room. I couldn't breathe. 'Excuse me, excuse me ...', I stumbled along the row, pushing past security, shoving the exit doors, running past the hundreds still waiting outside the hall, out, out into the streets of Manchester. I walked and walked for an hour or so, out of the city centre, dizzy and desperate for distance from the speech and the news machine that salivated around it. Collapsing into a doorway, I lay there on the tarmac for an hour or so before I could get up and limp my way back to the hotel.

News sobriety

The panic attack was followed by weeks of serious anxiety. I would wake with a clenched jaw and a feeling of impending doom, a sense of dread unfurling its black tentacles into everything I did: showering, dressing, walking to the bus. Although I had experienced anxiety before, this time there was little respite. Desperate for chemical relief, I sobbed in the GP's office but came out with nothing.

This hyper-anxious state – which began to ease after a few months – did, however, give me the gift of clarity, for in this time I developed a sudden aversion to the news. Initially I went to the news, as usual, for comfort and diversion. But as I scrolled and was assaulted by shouty headlines and the usual bile, I began to feel strong feelings of anxiety. The news wasn't a comfort. It was making me feel terrible. The snide debates on what was then Twitter drew feelings of mild nausea. Watching the shouty sensationalism on the TV news a feeling of tightness would start in my chest. It was too much. For the first time in my adult life I *just didn't want to know*, so I stopped. Just like that.

For four months I didn't actively seek out a single news item. Indeed, I went some way to avoiding the news. At home there was no scrolling or social-media browsing. At work I politely asked if we could switch off the TV news, which played incessantly in our office. As with weaning off any addiction, the more 'news-sober' days I had under my belt, the more I wanted to build on this achievement and the weaker the compulsion to check the news became.

Of course, if I was writing a statement for the prime minister on a breaking news story, I had to tune in – but it became clear that obsessively following the news wasn't necessary to doing my job well. When writing speeches about government policy announcements, I didn't really need to be refreshing news sites every hour; what I'd thought of as essential 'research' was actually a distraction.

During my months' long news fast, I had a surprising realisation: so much of my scrolling had actually been rather unenjoyable. In the same way that you might mindlessly eat a bag of stale popcorn despite the fact that it doesn't taste very nice, I mindlessly scanned dull, irrelevant or mildly irritating content because it was something to do. From the perspective of news sobriety this looked less like a regular treat for the brain, and more a tireless obligation.

Stepping out of the daily maelstrom of news gave me a clarity I had lacked for years. I realised that my attention is one of my most precious resources. My waking hours are finite – and I'm not frittering them away on news which serves no purpose, and which is only designed to make me feel angry, dismayed or outraged.

THE PALEO PRESCRIPTION
Free yourself from news addiction

Gorging on news is such a widespread addiction that most of us don't recognise it as an addiction at all. Yet recognising the fierce grip of news – and becoming more aware of the effect it is having on us – is essential to renegotiating our relationship with it.

You might start by noting how often you type in the name of a news website or scroll through X for the latest news. If you have a moment during a TV advert break, do you reach for your phone to find out what's going on? If you're on a train, do you skip from news site to news site, devouring the same story from different angles?

Start checking in with how this makes you feel. For years I was under the impression that I was enjoying my hourly dips into the raucous news-led debates on social media. Otherwise, why would I be doing it? But addiction doesn't work like that. Just because we feel compelled to do something, it doesn't necessarily feel good. So before and after your news catch-ups, pay attention to how it's making you feel: informed and energised – or anxious and irritated?

- Has consuming this news given me information that is productive to me?
- Has it uplifted me in any way?
- Can I do anything about the pain and suffering I have witnessed?
- Am I feeling better or worse than before I consumed this news?

Behold the outrage machine

As well as becoming more aware of how the news is making you feel, start paying attention to how it's *trying* to make you feel. In a busy, noisy world, one thing works to hook an audience like no other: outrage. We are baited to be angry and appalled at every opportunity, to rail at Karens or snowflakes, to rant about Republicans or 'woke' activists.

A research project which analysed more than half a million tweets to see which got the most retweets found that – surprise, surprise – the inclusion of words like 'hate', 'greed' and 'evil' significantly increased the chance of the tweet going viral. Using inflammatory terms like this increased the rate of retweeting by 15–20 per cent.[11] Start noticing all those news items or social media posts that get you going, and soon it becomes clear: the news is an outrage machine.

Have a news detox

My mini breakdown forced me to detox from the news because I couldn't look at it without feeling anxious. As an antidote to the relentless angry, outrage-inducing, impotence-inspiring news I'd been consuming, I yearned for the gentle and the calming: 1970s folk documentaries, online tutorials on wicker-basket weaving, anything featuring David Attenborough.

This full and complete break made me realise that I could skip the news without missing out. I felt lighter, less encumbered. For these reasons I'd encourage anyone to try a news detox, for at least a month.

For those used to checking news sites ten times an hour, a complete news detox can be hard to stick to. To make life easier – and ask less of your willpower – a sensible first step might be to imprison your technology (see Chapter 3). At a time when smartphones are treated as an extra limb, this might sound extreme, but having a physical barrier between yourself and your phone provides the distance you need to ask: is reading the news going to leave me feeling refreshed or irritated?

As with any addiction, it's helpful to hold yourself accountable by sharing what you're doing with someone you know. Don't bore on about your virtuousness, but let them know you've done another day news-free and it will keep you going.

What you will find if you live this way is that if the news is relevant to you, it will reach you. Big stories break out of the pages and into conversation. A tax rise, a terrorist attack, floods nearby: unless you are living as a hermit, all these things will reach you, even if you never read the news.

A friend who is a reformed alcoholic told me that the most important part of maintaining her sobriety was knowing the triggers that led her to alcohol and then avoiding them. Those triggers were hunger, anger, loneliness and tiredness, so as far as possible she takes care to avoid situations leading to these things.

To break news addiction, it can be helpful to pay attention to what triggers you to reach for your phone or switch on the news. Boredom? Loneliness? Free time with nothing to occupy it? If the urge to 'doom-scroll' is triggered by certain situations, try avoiding them.

Ration your news intake

If you do have a news detox, you might decide it's forever, but others will want to check in every now and again. To prevent the news spreading its addictive tentacles through your life, it can be helpful to set clear boundaries around how much you consume – and when.

The work I do as a newspaper columnist and weekly talk-radio presenter requires me to know what's going on, so I created my own weekly update. Every Friday I get a stash of three or four newspapers and read them. An hour or so is all I need to be informed for my work. Stories of any importance that have happened earlier in the week will still be making the papers by Friday. I've just bypassed a lot of distractions and trivia along the way.

If weekly news isn't enough, try half an hour or so a day: enough to keep abreast of the basics, but not enough to gorge on all the noise around the news. A friend rations his intake by curating a list of intelligent news-related podcasts that are only ten minutes or so each. Every other day he will listen to one, enjoying the brief hit of information but leaving it there. That way he feels up to date without being assaulted by random horrors or outrage-inducing clickbait.

If you're setting boundaries around the news, pay attention to *when* you're consuming it, too. Scrolling through terrible news first thing in the morning won't establish a positive mindset for the day. Doom-scrolling last thing at night isn't a great idea either, since activating our sympathetic nervous system (which gears up the body to respond to danger and stress) isn't the best way to wind down for sleep. Aim for sometime in the middle of the day instead.

Exit the echo chambers

When it comes to the news you *do* consume, it's a good idea to avoid those places on the internet that are designed to make you angry, smug, superior or outraged: the echo chambers where we love to have our opinions reinforced and our prejudices unchallenged.

Hanging out in these echo chambers might masquerade as intelligent debate or information gathering but really it's just festering in outrage and stagnating in our own opinions. Spending too much time in echo chambers can also, I have noticed, turn good people into news bores who think everyone wants to hear their latest rant. They don't! So whether it's X, Facebook or forums, recognise the sites that serve as your echo chambers and consider cutting ties.

Curate good information

We informavores hunger for information, so we shouldn't deny it to ourselves. Just feed yourself the good stuff. No, this doesn't mean consuming lots of news from quality sources that use impeccable fonts and make clever arguments. An alcoholic bingeing on Chateauneuf-du-Pape is still an alcoholic. Feeding yourself good information means carefully curating quality, enriching information to replace a lot of the news you've been consuming.

What do I mean by 'enriching'? It might mean something

that is genuinely educational. I adore *In Our Time*, a long-running BBC radio show. Each episode covers a wildly different topic – the writings of Marcus Aurelius; the Battle of Crécy; Citizen Kane – discussed by experts in the field. Listening to one of these shows I genuinely feel the grey matter expanding, but the information we curate for ourselves doesn't have to be challenging. The mildest of documentaries or wildlife programmes can be enriching. The point is to have a stock of information that can satiate our Stone Age desire to know more things, without turning to *more* needless, noisy news.

Stone Age wisdom on . . . the news

- Driven by our ancient survival instincts to gather information, we've become a news junkie society, and it's causing untold anxiety and stress.
- We need to stop overloading our minds with misery, and focus instead on what we can personally affect.
- Try detoxing from the news for at least a month; you may be surprised at how much better you feel and how little you miss it.
- If you need or want to consume some news, ration your daily intake and avoid scrolling first thing in the morning or last thing at night.
- Leave the echo chambers that are reinforcing your prejudices or making you fearful.

- Feed your Stone Age desire to learn fresh things by curating a stock of good information that will entertain and enrich – without enraging you, too.

5

Work and Leisure

A few years back, Nike ran a TV advert that got the goose pimples pimpling. Stirring music plays as athletes run, jump and tennis-ball-thwack their hearts out. Over this a voiceover intones: 'Don't ask if your dreams are crazy. Ask if they're crazy enough.' They get specific: 'Don't try to be the fastest in your school ... be the fastest ever.' Yes, we are all potential Usain Bolts. All we need is a crazy enough dream (and a pair of Nike trainers).

The campaign is a good example of what you might call 'dream culture'. Its message: having a dream means you're halfway to achieving it. Its mantras: you can be whatever you want to be! Believe in your dreams! If you can dream it, you can do it!

This culture pervades modern attitudes to work. It's not enough to aspire to accountancy or sewage-plant operating. You've got to be the tech CEO, the Wimbledon champion, the platinum-selling artist, the person famous just for being famous: 86 per cent of young Americans aspire to be a social-media influencer.[1]

Alongside dream culture, there's the instruction to 'find your passion'. Fail to do so and we feel destined to become dull, grey drones who blend into all the other dull, grey drones that constitute capitalism's fodder. We're inspired to find work we love so that, as the saying goes, we'll never work a day in our lives.

And of course, it's not enough to have a passion, you have to make a healthy profit from it. It's not enough to enjoy making ice cream in your kitchen, you've got to go on *Dragons' Den* and get investment to get it on supermarket shelves. It's not enough to love playing guitar, you've got to be in a band, the band's got to get a deal, the songs have got to chart, the success has got to be lasting ... Hustle, hustle, hustle.

Alongside status, passion and pots of money, here's something else we expect of work in the modern world: purpose. We want our job to be the vehicle through which we can live a meaningful life, otherwise we panic that we are wasting our lives. The expectation of pride-inspiring purpose might be met by those working in UN refugee camps, but the guy working in the sandwich bar feels lousy because (he thinks dejectedly) what purpose is there in stuffing a sub roll full of meatballs?

These expectations lead to disappointment at every age and stage. The teenager who doesn't get excellent grades fears being mediocre, as though mediocrity were a disease. The twenty-something whose side hustle hasn't gone stratospheric already feels a failure. The thirty-something spends so many hours at the office that their kid mistakes them for the delivery guy. The middle-aged worker beats themselves up because they haven't found their passion and fear that they never will. The sixty-something retiree feels that now they don't have a job they don't have an identity.

As our expectations of work increase, so it asks more of us. We work late, we work weekends, we check email constantly, we allow work to creep into leisure time. Nowhere is the developed world's culture of over-work seen more starkly than in Japan, where a quarter of companies have people regularly clocking in over twenty hours of overtime a week. Amid widespread concern about this, the government devised a scheme called Premium Friday: once a month, workers are encouraged to clock off at 3pm. The trouble is that a lot of workers won't leave. So strong is the pull of the office that some have to be bribed with about $30 just to go home.

How we worked

Our over-wrought, over-thought, over-worked approach is a world away from the lives of our ancestors. You might imagine that those striving to live off the land 50,000 years ago were forced to work themselves into the ground, too: forerunners of the Japanese 'salarymen' who collapse on to a commuter train home at midnight. Not a bit of it.

In the 1960s a young anthropologist called Richard B. Lee lived for a month among the !Kung of the Kalahari. Over those weeks he conducted detailed research on how they spent their days – and the results were surprising. Although it had been assumed that hunter-gatherers' lives were an endless grind,

Lee found that the work of finding food took around fifteen hours per week. Adding domestic chores took the total up to around thirty-five hours a week, still far less than the average Westerner spends on working, commuting and household tasks combined.[2]

While working at their daily tasks, hunter-gatherers were literally hands-on. As Lee wrote: 'everyone worked and everyone used both hands and mind'. Those hands spent hours twisting, pulling, carrying, grasping, scrubbing; a symphony of physical and cerebral effort that few modern professions ask of us. Imagine a prehistoric woman making fire as the sun went down. As she worked the sticks, the world around her would have stilled, with nothing to focus on but that meditative movement until the first wisp of smoke curled up. Compare this to the 21st-century worker: hands performing the same old clicks on the keyboard, mind fragmented across the twenty different tabs open on their screen and the twenty-three unread emails in their inbox.

Work was broken up by naps or long stretches sitting and chatting in the sun. Leisure time was not some cherry-on-the-cake half an hour at the end of a long day; it was taken seriously, and for good reason. When finding calories takes effort, it's wise to conserve those calories for the jobs that matter to survival and reproduction: finding food, carrying water, raising children. Beyond these tasks it made sense to rest, conserving energy for the important stuff. In short, they had the work–life balance cracked.

The biggest difference between work in the Paleolithic era

and now? It was free of the expectations and anxieties we've heaped on ourselves. When your daily need was to find and feed, you weren't fretting about your purpose on earth because that was pretty obvious. There was no competition, no career ladder to climb, no dream job to hanker after, no stark dividing line between work that was paid and work that was unpaid. All adults – from the foraging grandmothers to lightning-fast young hunters – had an important contribution to make. Because of this, work wasn't a measuring stick you used to compare yourself to others. Self-worth wasn't built on success.

The endless hustling, the unattainable dreaming, the search for purpose through work; don't be mistaken in thinking that these are a natural part of the human condition. They're not. They are inventions of modern life – and unhelpful ones at that.

THE PALEO PRESCRIPTION
Put work in its place

Putting work in its place doesn't come easily to me. For a good ten years I was a workaholic. You know when Oliver Twist holds up his plate and says: 'Please sir, may I have some more?' Instead of begging for gruel, I was begging for jobs and commissions. I put almost all my waking hours into work or work-related net-working, because I was chasing the feelings that I was *sure* would come with success: perfect satisfaction, perfect self-esteem.

Driven by this belief I worked ridiculously hard for years, missing birthdays, anniversaries, a couple of weddings. In one three-year period I did not take a single holiday. At my desk for twelve or fourteen hours a day, I barely saw sunlight. My skin was the colour of uncooked scallops. Friendships fell by the wayside.

Whatever I achieved, that feeling of 'making it' eluded me. I wrote speeches for the mayor of London; got a prime office in 10 Downing Street; shook the hands of presidents; featured on lists of influential people; collected an OBE; wrote a weekly column in *The Times*; started a business that did reasonably well. No matter the achievement, the old internal dissatisfactions needled me. *Where's the buzz? What's next?*

When you're busy hustling, you imagine the satisfaction and self-esteem you'll feel when you reach an admired level. But it's like chasing a rainbow. As a child you imagine how amazing it would be to get up close to a rainbow, inches from its vast, shimmering ribbons of red, orange, yellow, green . . . Then you discover that this is impossible. The beauty is only visible from a distance. Likewise, the perfect ego-trip promised by a dream job disappears on getting it – in my experience, anyway.

As with so many other things I write about in this book, I developed a realisation that my yearning for career success was a modern seduction that didn't serve my happiness as a human being. So, for years now I have been trying to keep work in its natural place, as a means to an end – rather than a cornerstone of my identity and the sole repository of all my ambitions. One of my stranger tactics for achieving that is to view my life through the lens of my death.

The living obituary

Nineteenth-century businessman Alfred Nobel invented dynamite, opened several explosives factories and made a lot of bucks for his bangs. He was mooching along happily until a life-transforming error was made. When his brother Ludvig died, a French newspaper printed an obituary about the wrong brother. Thus Alfred — very much alive — was able to read his own obit. It was ugly. 'The merchant of death', he was dubbed, a man enriched by developing new ways to 'mutilate and kill'. Horrified to think he would be remembered this way, Alfred left his vast fortune to create a different legacy: the Nobel prizes. A name once linked with war is now synonymous with peace.

A mid-life obituary can be a course corrector that points to the way you *really* want to live your life. That's why every now and then I write my own obituary. Although I don't plan on dying any time soon, imagining my life from the perspective of its end is helpful in clarifying what matters, and particularly, how work should be prioritised (or de-prioritised).

Do I really want the main item on my obituary to be that I was promoted a couple of times? Do I want to add that I made an extra £15,000 a year and busted a gut for it? Or do I want my obituary to be full of adventures, exploration, interests, and above all – relationships?

In these obituaries, Clare was someone who started a charitable enterprise that helped people. She was known for generosity with her time. She spent years living by the sea. In her later years she enjoyed all sorts of adventures: trekking through Madagascar, following her ancestor's journey to the source of the Nile. I admit that this Clare bears little relation to me at the moment. Maybe she never will! But thinking of the woman I *might* become helps me think about what I need to be prioritising now. And guess what? It's rarely work.

Writing a living obituary is a chance to tune out the modern noise about what makes a 'successful' life and tune in to what really matters – and if doesn't seem too morbid, you could try it yourself.

Write your own obituary

This isn't a test of writing skill. It doesn't need to be moving or profound; it's probably for your eyes only, after all. What this should capture is how you'd like to be remembered. Try to keep within the realms of possibility; coming up with a cure for cancer isn't realistic for most. Above all, be honest about what a rounded life looks like to you. Fast-forward in time and ask, from the strange perspective of your own ideal obituary:

- How did I spend my life, from beginning to end?
- What brought me joy?
- What were my greatest achievements?
- What qualities defined me as a person: was I energetic, empathetic, kind, stubborn, curious, easy-going?

- What mark did I leave on other people's lives?
- What values will I be remembered for?

Get hands-on

Winston Churchill: war leader, legend ... bricklayer. In September 1928 he wrote a letter to Prime Minister Stanley Baldwin talking about the 'delightful month' he had spent 'building a cottage and dictating a book: 200 bricks & 2,000 words a day'. Photographs show him busy at this pursuit, trowel in hand. Although there is no record of why he took up this hobby, I reckon that in his infinite wisdom Churchill realised that human beings have an innate need to undertake practical, hands-on tasks.

For hundreds of thousands of years, our ancestors spent much of their day using their hands in purposeful effort: crafting, building, threading, kneading, pulling, turning, twisting. Neuroscientist Kelly Lambert argues that using our hands to create tangible outcomes activates something she calls the 'effort-driven rewards circuit', which links the parts of the brain that control movement, thought and emotion. 'We're programmed to experience satisfaction and a sense of wellbeing after we exert meaningful effort,' argues Lambert, because our lives once depended on it. 'Even though our lifestyles have changed radically, it's reasonable to assume that we have retained the innate need for effort-driven rewards.'[3]

I first realised the hand–mood link at twelve years old. I was feeling down. My mother had taken me to the GP where (surprisingly) they had suggested anti-depressants. I refused. When we came home from the doctor's, my mother asked me to help her make the dinner, as we had a crowd to feed that night. She handed me a small many-bladed slicing tool and a huge pile of runner beans. Slice them, she instructed, so I did. Taking each fat green bean, pushing its end onto the five blades of the instrument so that the bean frayed at one end. Pulling those strips through and tossing them on to the growing pile of bright green beans. I did this over and over again. When I came to the end of the pile I realised that while my hands had been busy on my task, the tight knots in my mind had loosened a little.

In recent years I've become convinced that, as Lambert argues, working with our hands brings significant mental benefits. Alas, our mechanised, technologised world doesn't give us too many opportunities to undertake practical work with our hands. I believe we humans have an innate need to use our hands productively far more often than we tend to do now. So, several times a week I do something hands-on and practical. A dose of doing, if you like.

Painting the walls is a favourite dose of doing. My modestly sized semi-detached is like the Forth Bridge; pretty much as soon as I've finished painting one room I'm reaching for the paintbrush again. At least once a year every wall, skirting board and length of coving will get a new coat. This isn't expensive (I use cheap paint) and it is immensely satisfying, a hands-on counterpart to the computer-based work I do most of the time.

Try a dose of doing

See those things on the end of your arms? Hold them out in front of you. Unfurl the fingers. Make them stretch as straight and taut as the strings on a bow. Make them crawl like the tentacles of a many-tentacled creature. Make like Liberace and dance them lightly over an imaginary keyboard.

A dose of doing is about reintroducing ourself to our hands. It employs them in creating, crafting, building, threading, kneading, producing – all of these lighting up pathways of pleasure in the brain.

You're unlikely to be sharpening sticks and digging through the rocky earth to retrieve some tubers for your dinner, but there are plenty of domestic or creative tasks that provide the hands-on boost that our brains crave:

Painting walls

Gardening

Vegetable patch tending

Furniture upcycling

Food preparation: chopping, slicing, shelling

Bread making

Wall building

Repairing and restoring around the home

Sewing and mending

Knitting

Cleaning

Pottery

Take leisure seriously

In 1931 economist John Maynard Keynes wrote a famous essay called 'Economic possibilities for our grandchildren'. In it he predicted that by the 2030s, we would all be working a fifteen-hour week, with an abundance of leisure time. Although on the current trajectory this is off the mark, Keynes was prophetic about how difficult it would be for humans to submit to more leisure time because 'we have been trained too long to strive and not to enjoy'.[4]

Since the second half of the 20th century, average leisure time has declined. Even when we're meant to be 'relaxing', modern technology means that work creeps in. Twenty years ago white collar workers left their computers behind in the office when they went home in the evening, now they're working on the train, nipping upstairs to take a call, checking emails while watching TV. The hard and fast boundaries between work and leisure have been obliterated by technology.

Meanwhile, having little leisure time has become a status symbol. Talking about how you never get a holiday is a way of humble-bragging that you're too important for time off. This attitude was captured in a 2014 commercial by General Motors for Cadillac cars, aired in the US. In it, a wealthy man boasts about why America is great: while 'other countries work, they stroll home, they stop by the café, they take August off ...' Americans are 'crazy, driven, hard-working believers' who work late and take only two weeks off a year.

This is far from the approach of our ancestors. Judging by the habits of modern-day hunter-gatherers, they took leisure seriously. A group of researchers from Cambridge University lived among the Agta of the Philippines and observed how they spent their days. On average, adults spent twenty-four hours a week on out-of-camp work, twenty hours on domestic chores and a whopping thirty hours of daylight on leisure time.[5] Many anthropologists have observed how much of the day hunter-gatherers spend chatting or napping or playing. The lesson: a hard boundary between work and leisure matters.

How to carve out leisure time

- Re-frame the importance of leisure. Remember that you don't just 'deserve' leisure time as a treat, you also need it to function well.
- Schedule time out of the workplace. If you are allowed a full hour's lunch break, take it. Leave the building. Eating a sandwich al desko and flicking between work emails and your phone is not quality leisure time.
- Beware work–leisure creep. Just as you discipline yourself not to check emails at home, try to discipline yourself not to check 'fun' stuff while at work. It all turns into a grey area of less productive work and less fulfilling leisure.
- Establish a leisure Sabbath. Once a week, have a clear twenty-four hours with no work or checking emails.
- Imprison your technology. I've written earlier in this book

about how and why I imprison my technology; if your evenings are being taken over by work emails, it's a good thing to try.

Stone Age wisdom on . . . work and leisure

- Stone Age work offered the satisfaction of completing hands-on tasks without the status anxiety that so often accompanies our jobs today.
- Critically, hard work was counter-balanced with meaningful leisure time.
- Try re-framing the place of work in your life, rejecting the expectation that what we do for money should define, inspire and excite us.
- Remember that it's OK for work to be a means to an end – financial survival – and to find things which feed our passions and desire for purpose elsewhere.
- Indulge your Stone Age 'effort-driven rewards circuit' with regular doses of doing, undertaking practical tasks with your hands.
- Take leisure seriously, insisting on firmer boundaries between work and home.

6

Body and Movement

Every morning, prisoner 46664 woke at 5am in a two metre-square cell and carried out the same fitness routine. Whether the day was stiflingly hot or freezing cold he would run on the spot for forty-five minutes, followed by one hundred push-ups, two hundred sit-ups, fifty knee-bends and various flexibility exercises. Why? Because, explained Nelson Mandela, 'Exercise dissipates tension, and tension is the enemy of serenity.'

Many will recognise what Mandela was talking about. We swim, cycle, joust and jab not only to keep fit but also to stay calm, or to stave off the demons that would otherwise plague us. One study found that a brisk half-hour walk a few times a week was more effective than taking an anti-depressant.[1]

The majority of us know all this. We know that physical activity is good for body and mind. Alas, the majority do not have Mandela-like levels of discipline. How many dumb-bells lie gathering dust under the bed? How many bus journeys are taken for a few hundred yards? How many shoppers scan the car park for the space right next to the supermarket entrance? A recent survey found that just one in twenty Britons do the weekly amount of exercise recommended by the National Health Service.[2] Over twelve million adults in England undertake less than thirty minutes of moderate physical activity a week.[3]

It won't surprise you to learn that this is in stark contrast to hunter-gatherers. Our ancestors moved throughout the day: walking miles to dig tubers or hunt before hauling an 80kg antelope back to camp. Firewood had to be gathered, water lugged and stone tools hewn. In an age before slings and buggies, children were carried around until they were three or four, with the typical Stone Age mother covering upwards of 4,800 kilometres with the child in their arms over that time.[4] Some have even argued that ancient hunter-gatherers practised persistence hunting: chasing animals for long distances at moderate speeds until the animal dropped not from an arrow's sting but from sheer exhaustion.

'Ah', you're thinking: 'I know how this chapter's going to go. It's going to be a lecture about how lazy we are compared to our ancestors, a ten-page-long scolding to get your lazy self off the sofa and start running twenty miles a day.' On the contrary. The problem isn't that modern humans are lazy; it's that the whole *concept* of exercise goes against the grain of our Stone Age instincts.

Exercise vs movement

If you were to drop a hunter-gatherer into the modern industrialised West, one of the things they would find most peculiar is the idea of exercise as something separate from everyday living. They would marvel at the way we sit down at a desk for nine hours before heading to a malodorous gym where we run on a treadmill for half an hour, staring at a screen.

For hunter-gatherers, physical activity wasn't some grim bolt-on, it was threaded throughout life. The need to find and feed required a range of movement throughout the day: digging, carrying, walking, ducking, squatting, balancing, jumping, crawling, throwing. Movement was not a solitary pursuit but a social one, tribe members heading out together to forage and hunt.

In a study observing the Hadza, forty-six adults wore heart monitors over four two-week periods, covering rainy seasons and dry. The women spent hours digging into rocky ground with sharpened sticks looking for tubers to eat, often with a baby strapped to their back. The men walked for miles on the hunt for giraffes and zebras. On average, they were engaged in moderate to vigorous physical activity for two and a quarter hours a day – over *fourteen times* as much activity as Americans taking part in similar studies.[5]

Walking long distances is a central feature of their lives. The average male hunter-gatherer notches up 14.1 kilometres a day; for women it is 9.5 kilometres.[6] Each year they're walking 4,307 kilometres, roughly the equivalent distance of London to the North Pole. In contrast, the Brits who walk the most on average – women in their thirties – walk around 407 kilometres a year; roughly the stretch from London to Newcastle.[7]

Another key feature of hunter-gatherers' movement patterns

is variety. Anthropologist Dr Kim Hill, who spent decades living among the Aché hunter-gatherers of Paraguay, describes how 'they do moderate days most of the time, and sometimes really hard days usually followed by a very easy day'. For Hill, the hunt was a high-intensity workout: 'ducking under low branches and vines about once every twenty seconds all day long, and climbing over fallen trees ... I was often drenched in sweat within an hour of leaving camp.'[8]

Cave potatoes

But here's the critical point: although hunter-gatherers certainly did (and do) move a lot more than we do, they did this not because they were naturally more industrious but because they *had* to move in order to survive. Whenever they had the opportunity to do very little, they grabbed it, because squandering hard-earned energy on purposeless exertion would have been madness.

Think of how effortful it was to find calories. Hunter-gatherers couldn't just gulp down a bowl of cereal to fuel the morning jog; they had to spend hours digging into hard ground or hunting. Spending this hard-earned energy on non-essential physical activity made no sense. If there was ever an instinct to squander five hundred calories on a five-mile fun run, natural selection would have put paid to it.

Undertaking any physical activity when it wasn't necessary to survive or reproduce was, in evolutionary terms, a pretty stupid thing to do. They would have rested wherever possible. Thus, a powerful instinct to conserve energy whenever possible became hardwired into our genetic inheritance. The couch potato instinct goes back to our cave potato ancestors.

The curse of convenience

Next time you're beating yourself up because the sofa is more appealing than the treadmill, give yourself a break. You're not a flawed human, you're *being* human. We evolved to conserve energy, to be 'lazy' when the opportunity arose. The trouble with the modern world is that it offers *too many* opportunities to be lazy.

Instead of hauling water from a river, we can turn a tap on. Instead of collecting firewood, we can turn up the thermostat. Instead of walking long distances, we can get in a car. Instead of foraging for food, we can pop to the supermarket or, if we can't be bothered to do that, we can get a delivery to our home. Instead of taking the stairs, we can take a lift. We even have labour-saving devices for labour-saving devices: for those who don't fancy pushing around a vacuum cleaner there are now robot vacuum cleaners that silently cruise across carpets sucking up crumbs.

That in-built instinct to do as little as possible has been massively over-indulged by convenience culture. Modern life lets us off the movement hook, meaning many of us move little. Because we feel guilty about moving little – and because we know the benefits of physical activity – we resolve to get more exercise: the Zumba class is booked, the new swimming goggles bought.

I have, for short periods in life, been one of those exercise evangelicals who will bore on to anyone willing to listen about how my daily run has changed my life. I have felt the ecstatic feeling that comes around mile two, when your legs feel like unstoppable well-oiled pistons. I know how a bout of exercise can feel like taking a weary brain and injecting it with energy.

The trouble is that – for me as well as many others – the exercise habit doesn't stick. One day I'm fantasising about running the Marathon des Sables, the next I'm finding excuses not to put on my brand-new trainers. I used to berate myself for being terribly lazy, but now I know it's the Stone Age energy-conserving instinct. Although we do keenly want to be fit and healthy, a prehistoric voice is whispering in our ear that it's better to sit tight – and for most of us, modern working life gives us the opportunity to do just that.

The new smoking

For a few years in my early thirties I lived with a golf ball stuck up my back passage. At least that's what it felt like. I had coccyx pain, pelvic pain, all sorts of pain. I spent literally thousands of pounds on treating it: buying wedge-shaped cushions, investing in a ruinously expensive ergonomic chair, trying reiki and reflexology. I went to physios who would release the knots in my pelvic floor; osteopaths who thought the problem was with my gait; chiropractors who acupunctured the offending areas. One doctor prescribed oestrogen. Another suggested pudendal nerve block injections. Another thought botoxing my private parts might be the answer (no thanks).

In the end there only was one cure. After five years of working in 10 Downing Street, I quit my job, taking a few weeks off to re-group and have a long-overdue holiday moseying around Spain. It was under an ornate arch in the Alhambra that I realised I'd been pain-free for days. All of a sudden I realised what the problem had been. Like the denouement in a crime drama, the spotlight fell on the cause of all that discomfort: my old office chair.

For five years I had spent around twelve hours a day sitting at my desk. My behind was glued to my seat for the vast majority of my waking life. Why hadn't I worked out that this was the problem? Because sitting for large chunks of life is the norm. The average office worker racks up ten hours of sitting a day.[9] Between 1961 and 2005, the total time that Britons spend being sedentary increased by around 50 per cent.[10]

Sitting has been called 'the new smoking'. Although this sounds dramatic, there *is* a wealth of evidence linking prolonged sitting to diabetes, depression, heart problems, obesity, dementia, musculoskeletal problems, and even cancer.

Did hunter-gatherers never succumb to the buttock-relieving appeal of a mossy rock? Of course they did. The time modern foragers spend in relaxed, non-standing poses is similar to ours; almost ten hours a day. But critically, this time is broken up reg-ularly. They aren't sitting in front of a screen almost unmoving for hours on end.

The other critical difference is *how* they sit. Instead of letting the chair take the strain, much of their inactive time is spent squatting or kneeling, 'active rest' postures that require more muscle activity than sinking into an armchair.[11] This different approach to sitting can be read in the bones of our ancestors. Going back to *Homo erectus* – millions of years ago – you find little smooth patches on the ankle bones known as 'squatting facets', which indicate that the person in question spent a lot of time squatting.[12]

Whereas squats are now normally the preserve of gym bunnies, for most of our time on earth this was just how humans sat. In the 1950s, anthropologist Gordon Hewes studied postures of people from 480 cultures, including thirty-four past societies whose habits had been captured in artwork. He observed that 'a fourth of mankind habitually squats . . . and the rest of us might squat this way too if we were not trained to use other postures beyond infancy'.[13]

The hunter-gatherer health span

This is the hunter-gatherer pattern of movement: moving throughout the day, outside and with others; mixing up low and moderate-intensity movement with the odd burst of vigorous activity; sitting for short periods; squatting a lot, resting a lot.

This pattern serves the human body very well. Although it is true that those in the West live for longer on average than modern foragers (thanks to the marvels of modern medicine), it is also true that for many, death is preceded by years of poor health. Our life spans might beat the foragers, but our 'health spans' – the years we live without suffering chronic conditions such as cardiovascular disease or type-2 diabetes – do not.

Among hunter-gatherers, health and strength persists long into old age, with men and women in their sixties and seventies having the stamina and speed of Westerners decades younger. One study found that the average seventy-something Hadza woman walks faster than the average American woman under the age of fifty.[14] Among the Tsimané – a hunting, fishing and farming tribe in Bolivia who generally walk around 15,000 steps a day – an astonishing 65 per cent of over 75-year-olds had a coronary artery calcium (CAC) score of 0, making their risk of having a heart attack close to zero.[15] In industrialised societies, coronary artery calcification is present in 90 per cent of men over seventy and 67 per cent of women over seventy.[16]

Another study looking at the skeletons of ancient hunter-gatherers found that constant physical activity had given them bones as strong as those of orang-utans. Since the dawn of agriculture, our skeletons have become much lighter and more fragile, prone to breakages and osteoporosis. One of the authors concludes: 'sitting in a car or in front of a desk is not what we evolved to do'.[17]

Should we be surprised that our bodies fare so much better on the patterns of movement we followed for 100,000 generations, rather than the patterns of movement we've followed for just a few? We need drastically less activity now to survive, but what of the activity we need to thrive?

THE PALEO PRESCRIPTION
Make your life move

We were made to move regularly, not for the feast–fast dynamic of sitting down for ten hours before almost killing ourselves on a cross trainer for an hour. As Herman Pontzer, an anthropologist who has spent a lot of time studying how hunter-gatherers move, says: 'Don't block out an hour ... put a bit of activity into everything you do. Forget this artificial distinction between exercise and life. Try to change things so that you're doing them more actively.'[18]

If you're a committed exerciser who loves your regular run, swim or spin, all power to you. This chapter isn't an argument against exercise. Most physical activity is good for you. But if you think an hour or two of exercise a week can offset the damage done by sitting still for epic periods, you're wrong. And the truth is that many of us are more likely to succeed if we commit to modest, regular movement rather than ambitious exercise regimes. For years now I have sworn off 'exercise' in the formal sense, and embraced movement instead.

Threading movement throughout my days has meant changing my mindset about the conveniences on offer to me. We have become accustomed to taking any shortcut available to us, looking for the easiest, quickest and most effortless way to achieve a task or reach a destination. But if you really want to make your life move, instead of looking for shortcuts you've got to look for long-cuts. You've got to de-convenience your days.

Instead of getting the bus all the way to the office door, I'll get off a few stops earlier and walk. Instead of getting a small supermarket trolley for the few items I need, I'll pick up a basket. Instead of getting the lift up three floors, I'll take the stairs instead. Instead of pushing a toddler half a mile to the park in a buggy I'll carry them on my shoulders.

The walking cure

A big part of this lifestyle is walking, walking, walking. What Forrest Gump was to running, I am to walking. I walk long distances on a regular basis, not from coast to coast like Forrest but three miles to the shops, almost a mile to and from my children's preschool, several miles between meetings. On a fine day I might walk a few miles to the station to catch a train rather than getting a taxi there. If I'm meeting a friend at a café, I suggest taking our coffee to go and walking instead of sitting in the coffee shop. If I'm on a work call, I'll walk around the block while talking.

Many of the greatest-ever thinkers, composers and writers prioritised walking. Beethoven took a long walk every afternoon. After dinner every night Sigmund Freud went on a vigorous walk around Vienna's Ringstrasse, his son recalling 'my father marched at terrific speed'. The composer Gustav Mahler went on a three to four-hour walk after lunch. At two o'clock every day, Charles Dickens embarked on a three-hour walk, returning, according to his brother-in-law, as 'the personification of energy'. Charles Darwin broke up his day with three walks. Tchaikovsky went for a daily walk that was strictly two hours in duration; according to his brother 'he had discovered that a man needs a two-hour walk for his health, and his observance of this rule was pedantic'.[19]

All those wise men made a wise choice. Walking is proven to make us less depressed. It increases our energy levels. It is even linked to greater longevity.[20] In Sardinia a community of elderly shepherds walk miles up and down rocky terrain every day, working their hearts, bones and muscles from morning until evening – and as a group, these shepherds are the longest-lived men on earth, regularly hitting a century.[21]

So instead of seeing getting from A to B as something that I need to compress into as small a time frame as possible, I see it as an opportunity to get more walking into my day. Far from a *waste* of time, there can be few better uses of it.

Where possible, I aim to walk on natural surfaces such as grass or rocky ground; walking miles on asphalt isn't what our bodies evolved to do. As for how far to walk, I try to aim for roughly the same distance walked by the average hunter-gatherer in a week – around 42 miles. Some days I will walk less, some more. What matters is not sticking to the same distance every day but sticking to the resolution to thread walking throughout life.

How to start and keep walking

Create your own walking map
Have a list of places that you resolve to always walk to: the

---

local shop, park, library. Make it a rule that whatever the weather you get there on foot. Re-calibrate what you consider an acceptable distance to walk for an errand. If my destination is within half an hour's walk, I will walk it, even if it is just for a loaf of bread. Remember, this isn't a waste of time but a brilliant use of it.

Set weekly walking goals

If we don't have some idea of how much to walk, it's easy for the Stone Age energy-conserving instinct to kick in, telling us it's better to stay put. The 10,000 steps goal is great, but it's not always possible to walk that every day. Besides, hunter-gatherers tend to mix things up, breaking up long walking days with rest days. For that reason I think in terms of a weekly goal of just over 40 miles. This is pretty ambitious; walking around 30 miles a week would still be a great improvement on the distances most people currently walk. Half of all adult Britons walk less than a mile a day.

Dress for movement success

For most of our time on earth we were dressed – or un-dressed – in a way that allowed us to move easily. These days we tend to wear movement-inappropriate clothing unless we are in the gym. I appreciate that some workplaces don't want staff turning up in tracksuits. But many of us – including work-from-homers – have the chance to dress for movement success. To get into an active frame of mind, I wear workout gear most days. Jeans have not made an appearance for years. If I have meetings, it's wide-legged trousers and smart-looking flat shoes, rather than high heels that are impossible to walk any distance in. I'm ready, in short, to move.

Grab high-intensity opportunities

Although hunter-gatherers' bread and butter movement is walking, there would have been many times when bursts of high-intensity activity were required: running from a cave lion, scrambling through thick undergrowth, butchering a buffalo.

Some might like to emulate this by doing HIIT (high-intensity interval training) or a CrossFit class, where intense bursts of movement are interspersed with rest breaks. Personally, I don't have the time or inclination to do formal exercise like this. Instead, I try to thread high-intensity movement throughout my day.

Achieving this means being imaginative about how we use life and its props as our gym; if I'm carrying one of my kids across a park, for instance, I might break into a run for a few minutes. It's about seeking opportunities to suddenly and swiftly exhaust yourself.

Sit less, squat more

The most important take-out of this chapter – aside from the benefits of walking – is how vital it is to break up the time we spend sitting down. We're not about to burn our chairs and sofas, but sitting in a more intermittent fashion is a big boost to human health. One major study looked at the sitting patterns of 8,000 over 45-year-olds and found that those who sit for one to two hours at a time without moving have a higher mortality rate than those who sit for the same amount of time *but* in shorter bouts.[22]

Our bodies didn't evolve to sit in the same position for long periods of time. So I have a rule: never sit longer than thirty minutes. If you're at a desk, you can have a timer to notify you when half an hour's up – cue a stretch or walk around. If it's time for a cup of tea or toilet break, make this an opportunity to move for five to ten minutes.

Another way to kick the chair habit is by standing or kneeling to work. You don't need to invest in a fancy standing desk if it's beyond your budget. Much of this book has been written on an IKEA chest of drawers. Again, it doesn't have to be all or nothing. I might sit for a bit then stand for a bit; the most important thing is not to sit for an hour or two at a time.

While working to break up your sitting, it's a good idea to weave more squatting into your day. At first this will feel very odd. Dropping into a squat is pretty unnatural – especially in the office – but the muscle-strengthening benefits of this posture are so significant that it's worth persevering through the strangeness and wobbliness until this becomes more natural.

To help build it into my day I find it useful to have squatting 'cues'. It started with the laundry. With four young children I'm sorting piles of clothes for around half an hour a day; now I do this while squatting on the floor, the laundry pile next to me. While my kids are in the bath, I'll squat down next to the bath to chat for ten minutes or so. When watching TV, if I grab a drink and come back, I might squat for a few minutes before reclining on the sofa. It's about building associations between squatting and various activities, otherwise I'd forget.

Stone Age wisdom on . . . moving your body

- In the Stone Age, grabbing every opportunity to laze around was sensible; today it's a disaster for our health.
- Modern convenience culture gives us too many opportunities to opt out of activity, resulting in a global epidemic of lifestyle diseases.
- We need to learn from hunter-gatherers: not treating exercise as a grim counterweight to sedentary lifestyles, but weaving movement throughout our days.
- Take several walks a day, aiming for at least 30 miles over a week.

- Weave the odd bout of vigorous activity into your life: breaking into a run, lifting heavy things, walking long distances while carrying shopping.
- Sit for no longer than thirty minutes at a time, and squat more.
- Move outside as much as possible: walking, running, climbing trees, hiking up hills.
- Socialise while moving; moving with others is a proven way of helping you stick to the course.

7

Feast and Fast

The American system of capital punishment allows those con-demned to death to choose their last meal. Murderer Robert Alton Harris consumed a twenty-one-piece bucket of Kentucky Fried Chicken, two large Domino's Pizzas, a bag of jelly beans and a six-pack of Pepsi. Richard Cartwright went for fried chicken, a cheeseburger, onion rings, sausage and cheesecake. Killer Lawrence Russell Brewer's request was for two chicken fried steaks smothered in gravy, a triple bacon cheeseburger, a cheese omelette with ground beef, one pound of barbecue with half a loaf of white bread, three fajitas, a Meat Lover's pizza, one pint of vanilla ice cream and a slab of peanut butter fudge with crushed peanuts.

Not many people ask for steamed broccoli in their final hours. Again and again the yearning is for cheeseburgers, French fries, pizza, ice cream. Such requests are testament to the seductive deliciousness of ultra-processed food.

In the UK, almost 60 per cent of our diets now consist of ultra-processed foods containing additives you would not be able to spell, let alone find in your own kitchen cupboard.[1] By the age of seven, the average British child is eating eighteen teaspoons of sugar a day.[2]

This has not happened by accident. You've heard of Big Tobacco, which got the world hooked on cigarettes in the 20th century, but what of Big Food, the group of companies which has been even more ingenious at hooking the masses on to their highly unhealthy, addictive products?

For a century, all who profit from ultra-processed food have been very clever at developing and pushing cheap, calorific products that we can't get enough of. They helped spread the lie that saturated fat is the root of all dietary evil, suppressing the truth that sugar is very bad for us. They laced biscuits, cereals, fizzy drinks and ice cream with cheap and nasty high-fructose corn syrup. They found that if there's less water and insoluble fibre in a product, we're less likely to feel full while eating it, so we eat more and bump up those profits. They even worked out that combining fat and carbs in a 1:2 ratio – the same as that found in breast milk – will make that chocolate bar or tub of vanilla ice cream irresistibly delicious.[3] Fiendish.

Big Food and me

It took me a long time to realise that the food and drink I was consuming was grinding me down. A 1980s child, I was an ultra-processed addict. Afternoons at the park with my dad meant Salt & Shake crisps washed down with Lucozade. Adventures in the playground: blue raspberry Panda drinks. Lunch at school: Trio chocolate biscuits. Summer evenings in the garden: Mr Men ice lollies. Saturdays at the shops: Push Pops that turned your tongue scarlet. Sundays at the grandparents: Bird's Ice Magic, a chocolate sauce that hardened to a crisp when drizzled over ice cream.

Over the years it became natural to punctuate the day with treats for the tongue: sweets and chocolates in childhood; fizzy drinks and burgers in my teens; creamy lattes and cinnamon pastries in my twenties. *Quelle surprise*! I began piling on fat. By my mid-twenties I could grab several inches around my middle. The tops of my legs rubbed together in hot weather. Swimming suits dug in, cover-ups on the beach became a thing.

Gaining weight was bothersome, but the real problem was the fatigue. I was eating and drinking to sustain my constantly flagging energy levels. I needed a coffee when I woke up, something sugary an hour or so later, crisps and a diet Coke late morning, a doorstep of a cheese and chutney sandwich at lunch, a cup of tea and a couple of chocolate biscuits to help me through the 3pm lull. If I was heading out for the evening, I needed an energy drink and some vodka to pep myself up.

My blood sugar levels were riding a rollercoaster from morning until night. The tiredness was constant. I went to the doctor, convinced that I had cancer (I didn't). On I went, dragging myself through the days with the help of sugar, caffeine and alcohol. I had enjoyed a long love affair with Big Food, but by my late twenties, when it became too uncomfortable to wear jeans and I was craving a nap mid-morning, too, I knew the jig was up. We are what we eat, and I was sluggish, bloated and knackered.

Stone Age appetites vs corporate greed

Was this my fault? Yes and no. So many of today's health issues are the result of a pitifully mismatched battle. In one corner of the ring, Big Food, with its labs working out how to maximise taste and consumption, its heavy-handedness on ludicrously addictive sugar and salt, its multi-billion-pound advertising assault on our appetites. In the other, Stone Age brains and bodies that cannot easily resist this relentless temptation.

Our ancestors' life-or-death need to seek and find enough calories every day has bequeathed us a taste for calorie-rich food. If a hunter-gatherer finds a honeycomb in a tree, they will devour it, sensibly, because those calories are valuable to survival. Sweet things taste so good because they offer a big hit of energy, and our brain rewards us for finding this energy source by making us feel good.

We remain programmed in calorie-gathering mode – but now we can gather those calories with dangerous ease, not chasing an antelope to exhaustion, but picking up a grab bag of crisps at the petrol station. The results are predictable. The world is almost three times as obese as it was in 1975. Food has overtaken tobacco as the leading cause of early death globally. 'Diseases of affluence' such as coronary heart disease and type-2 diabetes have soared over the past half-century. In the UK, diagnosis of diabetes doubled between 2008 and 2023.

In a world of plenty, convenience and unprecedented choice, billions of people are killing themselves slowly, mouthful by mouthful. The modern diet is ruining our health, so what did the Stone Age diet do for our ancestors?

The Stone Age menu

Good evening, madam, sir. Today's special: an appetiser of nuts and wild olives, followed by roasted deer rubbed in garlic and mustard seeds, rounded off with fig and wild berry salad dressed in the finest local honey ...

The prehistoric menu wasn't all cold mammoth flesh. Depending on the climate, terrain and season, our ancestors might have eaten hare, rhino, antelope, buffalo, armadillo, porcupine, fish, cockles or mussels, supplemented by root vegetables, nuts, berries, dates, plums, pears, apples, oranges and golden honey. For almost 800,000 years – and some argue even longer – humans have been using fire to roast fish and meat, making it not only more digestible but more flavourful.[4] Tiny charred remains on cooking pots suggest Stone Age chefs used herbs and spices to give their dishes a kick.

Although it's long been thought that our ancestors didn't eat grains, there's evidence that some did. In a southern Italian cave, archaeologists found a 30,000-year-old pestle-like tool smeared with swollen wild oats; researchers believe that water could have been added to make prehistoric porridge.[5] At a 14,000-year-old settlement in Jordan's Black Desert, archaeologists found some burned material that, on closer inspection, was found to be a type of local wild wheat, which had been processed into something like flatbread.[6]

Stone Age eating was varied, nutritious – and intermittent. For our ancestors there were days when an enormous carcass was there to be gorged on, but there were also days when the weather spoiled the foraging, or the prey eluded the arrow. Neuroscientist Mark Mattson, who has been studying fasting for twenty-five years, makes the argument that our bodies and brains evolved to function well even when we weren't eating for days or weeks at a time.[7]

This way of eating served our ancestors well, and certainly much better than the diets that followed the agricultural revolution about 12,000 years ago. Studies have found that all over the world – from the place now known as Thailand to the place now known as Tennessee – people got sicker and shorter after they took up farming and radically changed their diets.[8] Modern diets were a particular disaster for our teeth. When Buffalo Bill's Wild West Show came to London in the 1890s, a doctor named Wilberforce Smith was permitted to examine the mouths of ten Sioux Indians, who were part of the show. He marvelled: 'the perfection of these teeth was almost startling to one accustomed only to daily observation of mouths in a modern civilised community'.[9]

Prehistoric bones and teeth only tell us so much. To see how these diets affect the rest of the body, researchers look to contemporary hunter-gatherers, and it's clear that the age-old diet is amazing for our insides, too. Wise old Hippocrates reckoned that 'all disease begins in the gut', and modern science increasingly agrees. Our microbiome, with its 'good' bacteria, is linked to our immune responses, our metabolism, even our mental health. Across the industrialised world, millions of us pop probiotics to boost our 'friendly bacteria' and stay well. And where are the 'friendliest' microbiomes in the world? Yes, in the last exclusive hunter-gatherer society in the world.

Researchers from Stanford University found that while the average Californian has 277 microbe species in their gut and the average Nepalese farmer has 436, the average Hadza hunter-gatherer has 760 microbe species – almost *three times* the number found in Western guts.[10] Tim Spector, a professor of genetic epidemiology, spent a short period living with the Hadza, enjoying a diet that included high-fibre treats such as baobab fruits and wild berries as well as more exotic fare like porcupine. Within just *three days* his microbial diversity had increased by 20 per cent.[11] There can be little doubt that ancient diets did a body good.

Disaster strikes the human diet

For hundreds of thousands of years, human diets served human bodies well. Then, around 10,000 BCE, people in the Fertile Crescent (an area covering modern-day Jordan, Syria, Lebanon, Iraq, Israel and Iran) began growing the first crops on the first farms: emmer wheat, barley, einkorn – the ancestors of our cereals today. Cue Hollywood movie trailer voice: *things would never be the same again.*

After millions of years of a meat-and-plants diet, carbs became king. After the hugely varied menu *Homo sapiens* had thrived on, the human diet was swiftly reduced to a few different livestock and a handful of crops.

In some ways the agricultural revolution was a marvellous

thing for those living through it. Food supply became predictable. More mouths could be fed more easily. You were less likely to be killed by fang or claw. Populations boomed – but, at the same time, human health took a hit. Several studies have compared the bones and teeth of hunter-gatherers to the bones and teeth of Neolithic farmers who lived on the same land, hundreds of years apart. Time and again they find that the farmers were shorter and less healthy compared to their forebears, wherever they lived, whenever they existed and whatever crops they harvested.

Over and over again we see the same pattern: healthy populations meet modern diets and their health takes a nosedive. In the 1960s a team of anthropologists and nutritionists investigated the health of various traditional populations around the Pacific, from the isolated Pukapukans of the Cook Islands to the New Zealand Maori, who ate 'modern' food. After eight years, Dr Ian Prior, the leader of the research, concluded: 'the farther the Pacific natives move from the quiet, carefree life of their ancestors, the closer they come to gout, diabetes, atherosclerosis, obesity and hypertension'.[12]

In a more recent experiment, researchers swapped the diets of twenty African Americans from the US city of Pittsburgh and twenty rural Africans from KwaZulu-Natal. The rural Africans spent a fortnight chowing down on sausages and hash browns, the African Americans on bean soup and vegetables. The results were astounding. After just two weeks the African Americans' biological markers for cancer had reduced and their colons were less inflamed. Meanwhile the rural Africans' risk of cancer had risen.[13]

The writing is on the wall. We didn't evolve to eat this way. Our bodies are paying the price for the modern addiction to fatty, sugary, nutrient-poor foods. If we are what we eat, is it any wonder so many of us feel like junk?

THE PALEO PRESCRIPTION
Eat how we evolved to eat

You've probably heard of the famous Paleo diet. Its basic principle is that our diets took a wrong turn during the agricultural revolution. It argues that because our digestive systems adapted to eat the kinds of foods we ate in the long Paleolithic period, to enjoy optimum health we should eat like our ancestors and avoid any foods introduced in the last 10,000 or so years. In practice that means plenty of fish, meat, vegetables, nuts and seeds, but no processed grains or dairy, no legumes such as peanuts, lentils or beans, and certainly no processed food.

Although I broadly agree with this, I have a few problems with the Paleo diet. First, the word 'diet' suggests our ancestors all ate roughly the same thing, when this is nonsense. They ate whatever the environment they were in provided, as do contemporary hunter-gatherers. Whereas the Inuit of the Arctic typically get most of their calories from seals, narwhals and fish, the !Kung and Hadza foragers of Africa get the majority of their energy from plants.

The Paleo diet also assumes that our bodies are incapable of evolving to adapt to new food and drink, but this isn't the case.

For the vast majority of our time on earth, humans couldn't consume dairy beyond childhood without digestive issues. It was only around 7,000 years ago that some Europeans started to develop lactase persistence, meaning that they could happily drink milk into adulthood. Although 65 per cent of the world's adult population is still dairy intolerant, across swathes of the Western world tolerance has spread remarkably quickly. Our bodies are still, after all, evolving.

My biggest issue with the Paleo diet is that it's just too restrictive. We don't have access to all the foods our ancestors ate – and frankly, not everything introduced after the agricultural revolution is bad for us. Whole-grain food is rich in fibre. Dairy is an excellent source of calcium. Just because a food wasn't around much (or at all) 20,000 years ago, it doesn't necessarily mean it's unhealthy.

The Relaxed Paleo diet

For these reasons I don't stick religiously to the Paleo diet, as laid out in dozens of books and blogs. Instead, my diet might be described as 'Relaxed Paleo'. This concedes that as far as possible we should eat as our ancestors ate – but it also concedes that never eating cake again is a little extreme. Broadly, Relaxed Paleo means doing three things:

1. As far as possible, cutting down on the ultra-processed foods which would be unrecognisable to the Stone Age palate.

2. Eating a lot of good-quality protein: organic or pasture-raised meat and wild fish.
3. Eating a mountain of fruit and vegetables.

These are the basic rules I try to follow, but it's *Relaxed* Paleo because if I lapse every now and then, so be it. I adore pizza and refuse to banish it from my life. Every Monday it's our tradition to make a special pudding as a family, and I don't want my young kids to see their mother eating a handful of seeds instead. The key is that eating natural, whole foods is the rule, not the exception.

I'm also not fussed about eating certain foods that Paleo purists would baulk at; white potatoes, for example. For rigid adherents to the Paleo diet, these are a no-no because they are high on the glycaemic index, meaning that they ramp up your blood sugar more than, say, broccoli. But they also provide a decent dose of vitamin C, they're cheap and easy to cook. Oh, and potato starch residues were found on stone grinding tools in Utah, which are almost 11,000 years old, meaning our ancestors may well have eaten them too. So potatoes are on the menu for me (not French fries or crisps, though).

White rice is another grey area for Paleo dieters. It's a grain, which means some won't go near it, but unlike brown rice – a whole-grain that contains phytates, lectins and other things that the Paleo diet warns to steer clear of – white rice is basically pure glucose. For those wanting to lose weight, shovelling white rice isn't the best approach, but it's gluten free, it's quick and easy, so for me it's in.

Relaxed Paleo: my go-to and no-no foods

Yes foods	No foods	Sometimes foods
Meat: beef, chicken, turkey, pork	Bread	Grass-fed butter (high in omega-3 fats)
Fish, i.e. salmon, mackerel, haddock, cod	Pasta	Kefir (good for the gut and low in lactose)
Fruit, i.e. pears, avocados, strawberries, blueberries, oranges, apples, bananas, plums, grapes	Cakes, biscuits and pastries	Legumes, i.e. beans, lentils, peas, peanuts
	Crisps	White rice
	Cereal	White potatoes
	Soft drinks	Dairy
Vegetables, i.e. broccoli, onions, carrots, tomatoes, peppers, spinach, cauliflower, butternut squash, sweet potatoes, turnips, parsnips	Fruit juice	Occasional treats, such as pizza or ice cream
	Added sugar	
	Artificial sweeteners	
	Ultra-processed food such as ham, sweets or breakfast cereal	
Eggs	Beer	
Nuts and seeds: almonds, cashew nuts, walnuts, macadamia nuts, sunflower seeds, pumpkin seeds, pistachio nuts, pine nuts, pecan nuts	Wine	
Oils: olive oil, avocado oil, flaxseed oil		
Non-dairy milks: coconut milk, almond milk, cashew milk		
Hot drinks: coffee and tea		
Herbs and spices		
Honey		

Eating like this isn't always easy. In a world of glazed doughnuts and Big Macs, you need to give yourself all the help you can get to avoid temptation. Here are five essential things I do to stick to healthy eating:

Avoid the blood-sugar rollercoaster

Modern diets can cause our blood sugar to spike and crash multiple times a day. One minute you're flying high and whooping with delight, the next your blood sugar is hurtling towards the floor and your body's screaming for a biscuit. Sugar is the major culprit in the obesity epidemic, because it suppresses the hormone leptin, whose vital job it is to tell our brain that we've already eaten enough. By preventing this message from getting through, sugar makes us think that we're still ravenously hungry and in need of more energy.[14] In short, sugar is only going to sabotage your intention to eat healthily. Best to avoid where possible.

Get stocked on snacks

If you open your cupboard and it contains a chocolate bar and a grab bag of pickled onion crisps, you're not going to have much success eating like our ancestors. I try to have good snacks in the fridge or cupboard, especially protein snacks. Since these are much more difficult to come by than carb snacks (I won't eat plastic-covered protein 'balls' and bars), this involves a little work. Once a week I'll stick a lemon and some thyme in a chicken and roast it, giving me some leftover chicken to pick at in the fridge for a couple of days. Hard-boiling a few eggs takes ten minutes and these stay good in the fridge for up to a week. Other snack ideas include:

Toasted almonds
Mixed seeds
Carrot/cucumber sticks
Fruit
Egg muffins

Ditch the scales

The point of this way of eating is to feel good, to avoid the artery-fuzzing, brain-fogging effects of so much processed food. The point is not to lose weight. We might kid ourselves that we are climbing on the scales as a motivator, but regular weigh-ins risk derailing the best intentions. If you go up a pound there's a golden excuse to jack it all in, even if the pound was actually accounted for by extra muscle mass or fluid retention. If we obsess about the numbers on the scales changing incrementally, we stop thinking about the most important thing, which is how our food is making us *feel*.

Plan for success

As a terrible and unimaginative cook, I used to hate the daily puzzle about what we should eat for dinner. I don't want to make these decisions every day – and a lack of planning also raises the chance we'll just plump for a takeaway instead. So I go for the same meals on a regular basis. For years, Mark Zuckerberg famously wore the same style of T-shirt each day so that he wouldn't have to waste time making decisions about what to wear. I'm the same with meals. To clarify: I don't have the same meal every day; instead I have a few different weekly meal plans that I rotate. That way I know I'm broadly on the right Paleo track.

Relaxed Paleo: a week's meal plan

Monday

Lunch Chicken salad with olive oil, a handful of nuts
Dinner Baked salmon with vegetables and sweet potato

Tuesday

Lunch Jacket potato with spinach filling
Dinner Stir-fried beef, cashew nuts and vegetables

Wednesday

Lunch Leftovers from yesterday's stir-fry
Dinner Grilled chicken, celeriac chips and salsa

Thursday

Lunch Ham and onion omelette with avocado salad
Dinner Pork chops and vegetables

Friday

Lunch Mackerel salad
Dinner No-bun burgers and sweet potato fries

Saturday

Lunch Leftover burgers from the night before with salad
Dinner Coconut lamb curry and rice

Sunday

Lunch Roasted chicken, roast potatoes and vegetables
Dinner Scrambled egg, mushroom and avocado

Stop supermarket meandering

Supermarkets are full of traps for healthy eaters: the smell of the bakery section, gorgeous-looking glazed doughnuts, treats piled high. Online shopping is a marvellous modern invention which helps us bypass these temptations. For those who like shopping in person, go armed with a meal plan so you know exactly what you're looking for. Take a list – and don't go 'off-piste'.

Omega-3

Modern diets have had an impact on our brains as well as our bodies. Omega-3 fatty acids are vital to the functioning of the neurotransmitters serotonin and dopamine, which are in turn critical to mood, motivation and stress response.[15] We obtain omega-3 from animal sources, especially oily fish.

Although the hunter-gatherer diet typically includes a lot of omega-3 fatty acids, the typical modern industrialised diet provides nowhere near enough of it. To ensure that I'm getting enough omega-3, I eat a lot of mackerel, salmon, sardines, walnuts, and ground flax seeds – and to cover all bases I take a good supplement as well. If you're buying one, look for a brand that contains high levels of EPA and DHA, and preferably one where the oils are sourced from a single type of fish rather than a range of different ones.

Intermittent fasting

The Paleo diet is all about *what* we ate; another crucial difference between contemporary diets and those of our ancestors is *when* they ate. These days we have a strange view about how often we need to eat. We consume multiple meals and snacks a day, taking a cereal bar for the bus journey just in case – horror! – we should go hungry for half an hour. But we didn't evolve to graze constantly. Over the long hunter-gatherer epoch there would have been days of feasting and days of very little food. As a result, our bodies are hardwired to respond well to short periods of deprivation. Studies have found that fasting can reduce the risk of type-2 diabetes, fight inflammation, improve blood pressure, boost brain function and even increase longevity.

Although I'm not religious about fasting, most days I skip breakfast, so I'm going straight through from one day's dinner to the next day's mid-morning snack. Some people find it helpful to think in terms of an eating window: a span of hours in which you do all your day's eating, whether that's up to six, eight or ten hours. Whatever the approach, it's good to remember the Stone Age lesson that skipping a meal here or there won't harm us; quite the opposite.

Stone Age wisdom on . . . eating well

- Our Stone Age instinct to consume as many calories as possible has resulted in a global epidemic of obesity today.
- Get wise to the way Big Food plays on this instinct, rejecting the siren calls of sugar and ultra-processed food.

- Eat good-quality meat and fish, and a lot of fruit and vegetables.
- Draw up (realistic) weekly meal plans, shopping for them online to avoid the processed temptations in the supermarket aisles.
- Keep a good stock of Paleo-friendly snacks around to help with energy dips.
- Try intermittent fasting (if your health permits it), having a window of fourteen or sixteen hours in a twenty-four-hour period without eating.
- Don't become preoccupied about sticking to a strict diet or weighing yourself; our ancestors would have been grateful for sustenance, not obsessive about its effect on their body.

8

Sleep and Rest

A halo of light glows around the edge of the curtains. Dawn is pushing its way into the room, and I'm still awake. Up since 3am, I've been through all the tricks to lull myself back to sleep: meditating, deep breathing, mentally walking through all the rooms in my old school, thinking of cities from A to Z. Nope – I just can't sleep.

In my twenties I would sometimes wake in the night for an hour or two. I didn't just feel frustrated; I felt like a *failure*. I felt like a failure in my teens when I'd stay up until 1am writing terrible poetry and then lie in bed until 10am: a lazy, slobby failure. I felt like a failure in my thirties, after having children, when waking every day at 5am even though the children slept soundly.

Why? Because we have been bashed over the head with the belief that the pinnacle of health and wellness can only be achieved when we get eight unbroken hours of excellent sleep a night, taken at hours that society deems to be acceptable. This is the ideal, the goal, the standard we all measure ourselves by.

When we don't achieve it, we can feel wretched, even defective. What's wrong with me? What could be more natural than easily falling asleep into an unbroken eight-hour blackout?

Human beings have long obsessed over sleep. In Renaissance Italy the recommendation for a good kip was to smear dogs' earwax on your teeth. In Elizabethan England, to 'anoint the soles of the feet with the fat of a dormouse'. Readers of a 19th-century Scottish magazine were advised to wash their hair with yellow soap. Charles Dickens advised pointing your bed northwards.

The obsession is understandable, given the clear health benefits of getting enough sleep. While the sleep-rich are more glowing, sociable and sharp, the sleep-deprived are more at risk of stroke, diabetes, high blood pressure, kidney disease, heart disease and depression.

Sleep matters – but are we placing too much emphasis on getting it the 'right' way? Taking a longer perspective suggests so.

You're not a sleep freak

Middle-of-the-night-wakers can feel that they're failing at sleep – but for centuries it was normal for our ancestors to sleep not in one long uninterrupted chunk but two. Historian Roger Ekirch spent years combing through diaries, court records, stories, letters and plays from the early Middle Ages to the Industrial Revolution – and found hundreds of references to the 'first sleep' and 'second sleep'.[1] The time between sleeps was used to pray, eat, read, have sex, do chores. Evidence for biphasic sleep was not only found in Europe but in Africa, South-East Asia, Australia, South America and the Middle East – and as far back as the 8th century.

It wasn't until the 19th century that we abandoned the second-sleep model because, Ekirch argues, artificial lighting meant that people stayed up later. Given that workers still had to get up early in the morning, the night's sleep got compressed, people slept more deeply, and the break in the middle of the night was gradually lost.

The revelation that 'biphasic sleep' was once a very widespread thing should help middle-of-the-night wakers re-frame their feelings about the way they sleep. They're not freaks whose wake-fulness betrays the laws of biology; they are simply experiencing sleep as many of our ancestors did for hundreds of years.

Another group of sleepers who can feel like failures is extreme owls. My teenage late nights and lie-ins always felt sloth-like and even sinful, perhaps because I had paid too much attention in Sunday school: 'How long will you lie there, O sluggard? When will you arise from your sleep?' (Proverbs 6:9–11). I had failed to fit the sleep mould set by modern society. I was lazy, indolent, wasting the 'best part of the day' under a duvet.

Extreme larks can feel freakish, too. As we get older, we tend to wake earlier; my mother-in-law is regularly up at 5am. This can frustrate the early riser, because they feel as if they're failing to fit the mould. If the rest of the world is still asleep, shouldn't they be, too?

Again, a longer perspective helps to re-frame these 'failures' as just a natural part of the rich tapestry that is human sleep. In 2017 researchers spent almost three weeks studying how the Hadza hunter-gatherers sleep. Not only was night-time waking common, but – just as in industrialised societies – the young tended to stay up later while the old got up earlier. The combination of night-waking and staggered sleep times meant that in the whole three-week period, there were only *eighteen minutes* in total when all thirty-three tribe members were asleep at the same time.[2]

The study backs up the sentinel hypothesis, which proposes that in the wild, nocturnal threats mean that it's a pretty good idea if there is always someone acting as look-out. If at least one member of your tribe is awake at all times, the warning can be sounded when predators strike. In this way, 'poor' sleeping – whether night waking, sleeping late or waking early – should be re-cast not as a failure but as a remarkable evolutionary adaptation that helped us survive.

So important are the staggered sleeping times of the tribe that being a lark or an owl is actually a genetic trait.[3] We each have a 'chronotype', indicating the times of day we are naturally inclined to be awake or asleep. Longing to hit the snooze button is not some lazy failing, it's because you are programmed to be that way. If you're waking for chunks in the middle of the night, it's not because you're defective, it's because once upon a time such behaviour was necessary to watch out for fanged intruders.

If hunter-gatherers had spells of wakefulness, fitful sleep, late nights and 4am starts, perhaps we have nothing to learn from them, right? Maybe our sleep issues have nothing to do with our modern lifestyles, smartphones and sedentary ways, and are simply the way we're meant to be? Well, not quite.

How hunter-gatherers sleep

Although archaeologists have found the world's oldest bed – a 77,000-year-old mattress of grass and bug-repelling leaves found in a South African cave – we can't rewind time to know how and when our ancestors slept. The next best thing is to study the habits of modern-day hunter-gatherers, whose sleep has been largely uncorrupted by modern distractions and technologies.

The most comprehensive study looked at not one but three traditional societies: the Hadza of Tanzania, the San of Namibia and the Tsimané hunter-farmers of Bolivia.[4] Ninety-four people in these communities wore watch-like devices to measure the light they were exposed to and the sleep they had.

You might imagine that when sleeping without modern distractions they fell asleep when the light went down, got a good twelve-hour stretch and woke when the light came up again. Not so. In many ways the hunter-gatherers' sleep wasn't dissimilar to that observed in industrial societies. Like us, they tended to fall asleep around three hours after darkness fell, using their evening to prepare food, eat and make plans for the next day. Like us, they tended to sleep in a continuous chunk. Like us, they got between 5.7 and 7.1 hours of sleep at night – a range that is actually slightly less overall than tends to be found in industrialised societies.

There was one big difference, though: insomnia. Whereas up to 30 per cent of people in Western societies report chronic problems with sleeplessness, just 1.5 to 2.5 per cent of the hunter-gatherers experienced insomnia more than once a year. It's such a rare phenomenon that the San and Tsimané don't even have a word for it. No tossing and turning, no counting sheep, no anxious obsessing about the sleep they're not getting. What are they doing right that we're doing wrong?

Across all three groups there were three sleep habits that were remarkably consistent – so consistent that we can only assume that this is the way human beings in non-industrial societies have slept for a long, long time.

Sleep habit 1

They fall asleep as the temperatures begin to fall. Whereas we use central heating systems and thick bedding to protect ourselves from the cold, for hunter-gatherers the declining temperature plays a key role in sleep. As Jerome Siegel, who ran the experiment suggests, 'this temperature rhythm has been reduced or completely eliminated for most of us by our shelters and heating systems'.

Sleep habit 2

While their sleep times might be staggered, as individuals the hunter-gatherers go to bed and wake up at pretty much the same time every day. If rise-and-shine time is 6am today it'll be 6am tomorrow and 6am the day after that. There's very little varia-tion, which research suggests is essential for setting our internal circadian clocks.

Sleep habit 3

They wake before sunrise, getting the most light exposure at around 9am. While those in industrialised societies tend to spend those hours huddling under a duvet, commuting or sitting in an artificially lit office, hunter-gatherers are exposing them-selves to the sun.

These sleep habits – with a consistency that suggests they are age-old – have been disrupted over recent centuries. Central heating systems have disrupted natural temperatures. The pull of evening distractions such as the TV and the internet have disrupted consistent sleep and wake times. The dictates of our largely indoor, working lifestyles have disrupted the habit of seeking the light early.

Let there (not) be light

One of the worst modern sleep disruptors is artificial light. In the summer of 2006 a German Science TV channel conducted an experiment in which three women and two men (aged be-tween thirty-one and sixty-four) were sent to live in 'Stone Age' conditions for a couple of months.[5] By day they gathered food in the fields. By night they slept in huts. For eight weeks they had no access to modern comforts such as running water, mobile phones or electricity. The only source of light was a campfire outside the huts.

Researchers measured the participants' sleep–wake patterns before, during and after the experiment. Under Stone Age conditions, they extended their time in bed and asleep by almost two hours a night, largely due to earlier bedtimes (waking time remained pretty much the same). As soon as they were back in the real world, with evening television, brightly lit rooms and mobile phones, the participants' sleep went right back to normal.

Another interesting study was done among the Toba/Qom hunter-gatherers in north-east Argentina. Handily enough for research purposes, one of the communities in the region had access to free electricity while the other didn't, relying exclusively on natural light: just 50 kilometres apart in distance, but millennia apart in technology. Who slept the longest? You know the answer. The society with access to electric light slept around forty minutes less in the summer and an hour less in the winter.[6]

Electric light affects our sleep in all sorts of ways. It inhibits the release of the hormone melatonin, which is meant to ease us in to sleep. It confuses our internal circadian clocks, which govern when we feel tired. And it lets us engage in activities that are impossible in the dark, from tiddlywinks to cleaning out the cupboards. Light tells us that it's a time for *doing*, not sleeping. As Harvard professor of sleep medicine, Charles Czeisler, has put it, 'Every time we turn on a light, we are inadvertently taking a drug that affects how we will sleep and how we will be awake the next day.'[7]

The problem with light, and with inconsistent sleep times, or inconsistent temperatures, is that they mess with our internal timekeeping system: our circadian clock. This cluster of around 20,000 neurons is located in the hypothalamus. When it perceives certain signals – such as light – it sends out hormones so that the body can act appropriately for the time of day. When it perceives light in the morning, the circadian clock prompts the release of a load of chemicals, including cortisol, to wake us up and make us alert. At the end of the day, as the light fades, this is taken by the circadian clock as a signal to produce the hormone melatonin, which reduces wakefulness.

Light isn't the only signal that regulates our circadian clock; our body temperature, food intake, physical activity and social stimulation do, too. For millennia our circadian clocks were set – and we were lulled into slumber – by natural sleep regulators, from the campfire's glow to falling temperatures to the quiet that descended as conversations hushed and our fellow clan members fell asleep. Given that modern sleep disruptors – electric lights, smartphones, central heating systems, insulated homes – directly challenge these natural rhythms, it's little wonder that so many have problems with sleep.

THE PALEO PRESCRIPTION
Sleep the way nature intended

I had three babies in three years, so in those days I won the gold star for sleep deprivation. For years I was functioning on four to five hours a night. Living was like wading through treacle. You know when you pull the cord on a lawnmower and it refuses to start, just making that dull, defeated 'rrrrr'? That was my brain when I tried to do anything more complex than walk.

It's only when you come through a period of prolonged sleep deprivation that you realise how much it has affected you. Suddenly colours seem brighter, life easier – all because you don't feel terrible. As my children started sleeping more reliably, I decided to take my own sleep more seriously. Although I had for years been practising some good sleep habits (no caffeine, lots of exercise), I wanted to go further, emulating the habits of our ancestors, and ridding my life of the modern sleep disruptors. Here are my six essential steps to Stone Age sleep.

1. Evenings by candlelight

In the long evenings of prehistory our ancestors didn't just prepare for sleep with the setting of the sun: they had campfires. This glowy light – on the yellow end of the spectrum – is far more conducive to sleep than the blue-light-emitting devices and bright light bulbs that we use these days. So I started using candles in the evening as a way to calm my over-excited children before bed. When it's bathtime I light a couple (well out of reach) and immediately a hush falls over the bathroom. The children are transformed from wild beasts to silent figures in a softly lit Rembrandt painting. So striking was the effect of the candlelight on my children that I wanted the same magic for myself. Now, from about nine o'clock, everything in my house is done by candlelight. I love every bit of this evening ritual: striking the matches, smelling the sulphur dioxide, spreading the glow until the house is as atmospheric as a theatre set, with shadows thrown upon the wall. Best of all it sets the stage – and the melatonin – for sleep.

2. Stop the stimulants

To help me through the long nights of babyfeeding I installed a TV in the bedroom on which I could watch *The Real Housewives of Beverley Hills* while burping a baby over my shoulder at 3am. Even once the baby feeding was over I continued to snatch a bit of TV in bed every night, pressing the off button on the remote as my last act before slumber. This is, of course, a long way from the quiet conversations and final potterings that preface the hunter-gatherers' sleep, so I have now banished all devices – television, laptop, smartphone – from the bedroom. As discussed earlier in the book, my smartphone is 'imprisoned' overnight, replaced on the bedside table by an old-fashioned alarm clock. It's simply too tempting to have a final scroll through the smartphone before sleep, thus firing up our brains again, both with the light being emitted and the content we're reading.

3. Play it cool

Our hunter-gatherer ancestors slept in caves, huts or outside, where it got noticeably colder around bedtime. They didn't just sleep in lower temperatures, their circadian rhythm also reacted to the *declining* temperature. Thus a night-time dip in temperature still sends a primal signal that it's time to sleep. You can probably set fancy timers on your thermostat to make the temperature decline over a few hours but, for me, the best way to mimic the temperature-drop experienced by the hunter-gatherers is to turn the heating off entirely, allowing the temperature outside to set the temperature inside. Of course, if you have young children or babies, or elderly people, in the house – or if you're in the middle of a bitter winter – it is more sensible just to set the temperature low. I'm happy at around 16 degrees centigrade as long as there are warm covers to huddle under.

4. Black it out

I live in a suburb, which the local council, in its wisdom, has decided should be lit up at night like Piccadilly Circus. The glaring streetlights are, handily enough, right at the height of bedroom windows, which is a problem for sleep. One study found that those living in urban areas of more than half a million people suffer night-time light levels that are up to six times brighter than those in small towns and the countryside. The urbanites reported less sleep and more tiredness. Is it any wonder? I want the inky blackness that those in pre-industrialised societies enjoy, so I double up on blackout. As well as blackout-lined curtains I have blackout blinds that stick to the window frame with Velcro, expunging all the light from outside. Alas, I am not sleeping under a black sky pin-pricked with stars, but this is my best way of emulating natural conditions.

5. Have groundhog nights

It used to be that when I'd had a difficult night – sick children or 1am worries – in the morning I would make some incoherent noises to my husband which meant: 'Please allow me to lie in for another ninety minutes or so. I owe you one. Thanks. Zzzz.' Sometimes I was up at 6am, sometimes 7, sometimes half past 8 or 9. I thought I was doing my tired body a favour, but this inconsistency was confusing my circadian clocks. Hunter-gatherers wake at pretty much the same time every day, so now I do, too: 6.30. Never mind if I've been woken five times by children in the middle of the night, this is my time. After a month or so of this, I stopped needing to use my alarm clock. Invariably I wake within five minutes of this time, thanks to my well-oiled circadian clock.

I aim for consistency in the evenings, too, with lights out by 9.30pm. This isn't always easy; the owl in me often wants to start writing a book/baking a cake/working on a cure for cancer in those inspired evening hours, but I know that if I am consistent it's easier for my brain and body to get into a rhythm, teeing up the hormonal and neurochemical changes needed for sleep at the 'right' time, which for me is between 9.30 and 10pm.

6. Make time for morning glory

In an ideal world I'd wake with the sunrise each day but, living far from the equator, sunrise is a little too variable for that. In the UK, dawn comes as early as 4.45am in summer and 8am in winter. Although I won't be getting up at 4.30am to see the sun rise, I do make it an absolute priority to make time for morning glory – my name for the fifteen to twenty minutes I spend outside every morning, 'light bathing'. As soon as possible – and still in my pyjamas – I head out to the sun lounger I keep on our patio. In the spring and summer months I'll throw on a light jumper, lie down and gaze up at the light. In the colder months I'll put on one of those big fleecy outdoor changing robes that people tend to use after outdoor swimming. If it's blowing a howling gale, I don't light-bathe; sometimes the elements defeat us. But I certainly don't let the cold get in the way. In fact, a crisp and bright winter's day is my favourite time to light-bathe, a cup of lemon and ginger tea in hand. Start to do something like this daily and you will find that whatever the weather, your feet are taking you out of the door to do it. It becomes not just a ritual but also a need.

Morning light-bathing is good for us in so many ways. Getting at least a quarter of an hour of direct outside light in the morning is essential for setting our circadian clocks. Sunlight helps your brain to produce serotonin, setting the mood for the day. I strongly recommend giving it a whirl. If you love to be horizontal (as I do) an inexpensive sun lounger is a good investment for light-bathing. If you're having a light-bathe, try very hard not to turn this into a phone-scrolling time ... taking in the light should be a time of clarity and peace, not news reports and shouty social-media updates.

Of course, not everyone has a garden or balcony that they can light-bathe in. If you live in a flat, getting out into the light early might mean adding fifteen minutes on to your walk to the bus so that you can stop at a bench on the way, close your eyes and light-bathe. And although natural sunlight is by far the best tool for light therapy, for those who find getting outside difficult, a light box that emits artificial light is a good alternative.

Take the long view

When people become fixated on sleep issues, worry can reinforce the problem. If you feel you're failing at sleep – fretting that you're not getting enough of it, or enough of the right quality – remember that throughout our long time on earth, human sleep has been a tapestry of different durations, sleeping times and waking times. The eight-hour ideal is no one-size-fits-all. Realising this might, hopefully, bring comfort.

Stone Age wisdom on . . . sleep

- Hunter-gatherers sleep closer to the rhythms of nature, helping to set the circadian rhythms in their bodies.
- Seek out natural morning light as early as you can, tuning your body's clock for the day – and night – to come.
- In the hour or two before bed, cut out modern sleep disruptors such as television and smart phones.
- Try spending the later part of the evening in candlelight, or at least not bright artificial light.

- Keep your bedroom as cool as you can bear it, preferably with windows open so that the decline in temperature sends a sleep-preparing signal to your body.
- Aim for consistent waking and sleeping times every day to set your internal clock.

9

Sex and Attraction

A campfire 40,000 years ago. There is something about her; the way the flames' glow lights up her soft features, the plumpness of her lips, the arch of her back. He just wants to be near her, and she him. He is known for his hunting skills, often coming back with a feast for the band to devour. They are magnetised, entranced ... They pair up, have sex, have babies.

The scene around the campfire in 38,000 BCE is not all that different from the scene in the nightclub in 2024 CE. Then, as now, we were driven to seek mates who would give us the best chance of passing on our genes. Then, as now, women tended to be more attracted to men who could provide the resources they needed to help create, nurture and raise children. Then, as now, men generally prioritised beauty and youth in their mate choice, because these are proxies for fertility.

We might think ourselves sophisticated creatures who are un-bound by such primitive calculations, but the old gene-spreading urge is still felt in countless subtle ways. Take the fact that men with deep voices tend to be considered more attractive. Why? A study of Hadza women found that they prefer men with Barry White-style baritones because they assume that they are better hunters. Could this be at the root of our continuing appreciation of deep voices in the developed world?[1] Another oddity: women at the most fertile point in their cycle are three times more likely to wear red than those at the least fertile point, a subconscious choice driven by the age-old linking of the colour red with fertility and attractiveness (perhaps because of the way some women's skin takes on a rosier tone when oestrogen levels rise).[2]

Researchers have even found that men are particularly attracted to women with a back that curves *exactly* 45 degrees above the top of her bottom, because this precise angle would have given Stone Age women an advantage in pregnancy. As bellies grew, this spinal curve would have helped to shift their centre of mass back over their hips, thus allowing them to stay active and forage for longer.[3]

That such a tiny and subtle breeding advantage still causes the male pulse to quicken tens of thousands of years beyond its practical relevance underlines an important point: our sexual instincts are rooted in our Stone Age past.

Lessons from the prairie voles

Our hormones work in the same way today as they've always done: a cocktail of feel-good chemicals that draw us to a mate for the purpose of perpetuating the species. As we pass through the phases of lust, attraction and attachment, different hormones do their work.

During the lust phase, testosterone and oestrogen are stimulated in both men and women. During attraction, the hypothalamus fires out dopamine, explaining those feelings of ecstasy. When it comes to attachment, the two primary players are oxytocin and vasopressin. For evidence of the power of these hormones, look no further than prairie voles. Whereas their promiscuous cousins, the montane voles, are about as faithful as a drunken stag party in Las Vegas, prairie voles stay with their partners for life. Once they have mated, they have eyes only for each other. When one dies, they even show signs of a broken heart.

Why the difference between prairie and montane voles? Because prairie voles have higher levels of receptors for oxytocin and vasopressin. In an experiment where the promiscuous montane voles were dosed with these bonding hormones, they too became monogamous and loyal to their mate.[4] Oxytocin and vasopressin work in a similar way in human beings: they are hormonal superglue, binding us to our lover.

The 'casual' sex myth

Why is all this relevant in a world of hook-ups, dating apps, sexual choice and female empowerment? Because however sexual culture may change, our ancient hormonal responses stay the same. The denial of this truth has led to the creation of an unhelpful modern myth: that for women, there is such a thing as 'casual' sex, the idea that we can enjoy random or one-off sexual encounters in exactly the same carefree way that men can. This may be the acceptable 'sex positive' view, but it ignores the way that female bodies and brains evolved to respond to sex.

The poet Philip Larkin mournfully wrote that 'sexual intercourse began | In nineteen sixty-three | (which was rather late for me)'.[5] Nineteen sixty-three was around the time that the contraceptive pill became widely available in the UK. 'Up to then,' writes Larkin, 'there'd only been a sort of bargaining.'[6]

'Bargaining' might be an ugly way of putting it, but Larkin is pointing to the different agendas that governed human sexual relations since the dawn of the human race. If a man and woman had sex that resulted in a pregnancy, and the woman was left to raise the child alone, she faced a daunting task. Therefore it made sense for the woman to be choosy about whom she had sex with. Women's sexual agenda was to grant sex to those who could offer them commitment and resources to help raise the child. They limited the supply of sex. Men's agenda was to seek sex, to vie for women's attentions.

For millennia, the dynamic between the sexes was set. Then came reliable contraception. Within a tiny span of time, the rules of the game as practised for hundreds of thousands of years changed. Previously, women's sexual behaviour had been shaped by the possibility of unwanted pregnancy. Suddenly, they enjoyed a freedom that men had enjoyed since time immemorial: to have sex without the worry that its most obvious consequence would fall squarely on their shoulders. Although this was great news, it has also led to the unhelpful belief that women are a lot like men in the way they respond emotionally to sex.

Over recent decades it has come to be seen as pro-feminist to be promiscuous. Women who have sex 'like men' – enjoying casual encounters with multiple partners – have been lauded as liberated. In the first episode of *Sex and the City*, Carrie Bradshaw has a casual encounter with a man, after which she declares, 'I'd just had sex like a man. I left feeling powerful, potent, and incredibly alive ...' But while contraception can liberate us from old social conventions, it can't liberate us from hormonal responses which are far, far, older.

When human beings have sex, the hormone oxytocin is released. Remember the prairie voles? This is the one that bonds us fiercely to another. And guess what? Women produce far more of this hormone than men, which means that they are more likely to develop a deep attachment to someone after having sex with them. Many a time I've commiserated with a friend experiencing the agonies of 'why hasn't he called?' after an amazing night together. Sex has primed their brains for commitment with a man, but it hasn't worked the same bonding magic on the man involved.

As anthropologist Dr Helen Fisher says, 'it's entirely possible' to fall in love off the back of a one-night stand: 'there's no question about it, good sex is going to trigger the brain systems that push you towards romance and attachment'.[7] The truth is that for many of us, casual sex is an oxymoron. How can sex be truly 'casual' when age-old hormones are telling your brain that this act is a precursor to long-term pair-bonding?

THE PALEO PRESCRIPTION
Respect Stone Age sex drives

Sex-positive feminists argue that while men used to have all the fun, now women are owning their sexuality, enjoying shame-free 'hook-ups', feeling empowered. But our Stone Age instincts – and hormonal responses – mean the no-strings culture often isn't so 'positive' for women.

It's not empowering when a surge of sex-triggered oxytocin means that women fall for men who don't fall for them back. It's not empowering when women find that men are increasingly reluctant to commit. Professor Dawn Maslar has written extensively about the relationship junctures at which men and women start to feel seriously bonded to one another. For women, the bonding hormone oxytocin skyrockets when they have sex. For men it's different. While they are uncommitted to a partner, their levels of testosterone are higher, which actually blocks oxytocin. It's not until the point at which men commit that testosterone drops and oxytocin – that loving feeling – is allowed to rise.[8]

Broadly, then, women start bonding in earnest when they have sex; men start bonding in earnest when they commit. If the sex comes before any explicit commitment, different agendas will often lead to confusion and hurt. This is especially true in the online dating age, when so many sexual possibilities are out there via the swipe of a thumb across a smartphone.

For some this will all sound offensively generic: there are, of course, women who will be perfectly content to have multiple casual partners who won't commit, and men who are the human equivalent of the devoted prairie vole. There will be lots of couples who have sex on first meeting and who are now toasting their thirty-year anniversary. This is great, but in general a culture of quick-and-easy sex serves men's interests and inclinations better than women's.

Is this heading towards an argument for women in chastity belts until their wedding night? No! It's good that women are able to enjoy premarital sex without being (metaphorically) tarred and feathered as in the bad old days. What is wrong is for women to think that if they're not as gung-ho about casual sex as men, then they're cold or frigid.

The advice: if you're looking for a long-term relationship, consider delaying intimacy for a while. This avoids the risk of developing sex-induced feelings for someone who's not right anyway. It also lessens the risk of losing someone who's right if they haven't felt that commitment-induced surge of oxytocin yet. It might sound old-fashioned, but so are our hormonal responses.

Face some hardcore truths

In the 1950s, biologist Nikolaas (Niko) Tinbergen discovered that birds which laid small, pale blue eggs with grey speckles much preferred to sit on big, bright blue plastic eggs with large speckles drawn on them with marker pen. These fancy eggs he called 'supernormal stimuli': an artificially exaggerated version of something we find in nature, which triggers an exaggerated response.

What applies to birds applies to humans. When offered an exaggerated version of something our species has always craved, we are powerfully drawn to it. Hello, pornography. Our Stone Age survival instinct to spread our genes has been hijacked by the supernormal stimuli that is the $100-billion porn industry – and many are hurt as a result.

An army of couples' counsellors would testify that pornography often plays a role in relationship breakdown. Countless addicts would testify to the shame of living a life governed by porn.

The more pornography people view, the more they are de-sensitised to it. To get the same buzz, they've got to look at harder and harder material. In *Never Enough: the Neuroscience and Experience of Addiction*, neuroscientist Judith Grisel explains that as the brain gets used to frequent hits of dopamine, it starts slowing down ordinary production of the neurotransmitter.[9] The result? Just to feel 'normal', we need another hit of whatever drug we're taking: alcohol, cocaine, orgies.

Desensitisation means that those who watch a lot of porn may start experiencing sexual dysfunction, too. Real sex doesn't cut it any more. And so the dopamine highs start being interwoven with inadequacy and shame. There's even evidence that porn use can change the structure of the brain. It is, in short, another part of modern life that isn't serving a lot of people.

Stone Age wisdom on . . . sex

- We're told that we've reached an age of sexual freedom: have sex with who you want, watch all the porn you want . . . but we cannot liberate ourselves from Stone Age sexual drives and instincts.
- Age-old hormones mean 'casual' sex is not casual for everyone.
- If looking for a committed relationship, try delaying intimacy for a while.
- Recognise that porn is a supernormal stimuli: an exaggerated version of something your Stone Age brain is craving and thus hard to resist.
- If pornography is damaging your relationships, sexual function or self-esteem, take steps to address it, such as blocking porn sites or joining one of the many apps which helps users to quit.

10

Love and Relationships

'Love is patient, love is kind' (1 Corinthians); 'love is a serious mental disease' (Plato); 'love is a smoke made with the fume of sighs' (Shakespeare); 'love is the flower of life' (D.H. Lawrence); 'love is space and time measured by the heart' (Marcel Proust) . . .

Never in the history of language has one word been so freighted with the expectations of billions of souls, saddled with the responsibility of giving our lives purpose, shape, meaning and joy.

We wrap love in wonder; even the most grounded people lapse into the language of the crystal ball when discussing it: it was 'fate', 'destiny', 'meant to be' . . . Two star-crossed lovers meet outside a kebab joint; later they marvel at the serendipity of it all: what would have happened if he had not felt compelled to go back in for some extra garlic sauce?

Given the lustre that romantic love adds to so many lives, we don't like to think much about the evolutionary roots of it all, because this hauls the work of 'fate' and 'destiny' back into the more prosaic realm of hormones and biology. It threatens to tarnish the magic. But so many of the disappointments and dashed expectations associated with romantic love are down to a denial of evolutionary truths, or at least ignorance of them. Taking the longer perspective – knowing *why* and *how* we human beings have loved and paired up for millennia – could save us a lot of heartache.

Why we love

Of all the definitions of love that have been written, novelist Somerset Maugham got closest to the truth: 'Love is only a dirty trick played on us to achieve continuation of the species.' Love began as a commitment device, an evolution-mixed hormonal cocktail which binds couples together long enough for children to be created, born and raised to independence.

In the context of our family tree, human monogamy is an odd thing. Fewer than 10 per cent of mammal species are monogamous. Our closest cousins, the chimpanzees, are highly promiscuous. Wouldn't this make evolutionary sense for us, too? Why has our species bothered with the whole messy business of love and monogamy when we could just meet, mate and part?

Promiscuity might seem a good gene-spreading strategy, but it has its limits. If a woman was left to raise a baby without a male, feeding the infant while gathering enough food for herself and others *and* dealing with the attentions of other men, that baby was less likely to survive. If, however, a father stuck around to help, that increased the chance that his children would make it, along with his genes. For Stone Age man, another benefit of pair-bonding was that you could be confident that the baby was yours, rather than some other bloke who'd had sex with the lady in question while you were away. And so, many argue, monogamous relationships were critical to the success of our species.

Grating expectations

Why should we care about the roots of monogamy today? Because it is in the conflict between age-old truths and modern culture that so much heartache is created.

In the Stone Age, pair-bonding was a practical arrangement for the raising of children. Today, bride and groom may stand at the altar and promise to be each other's 'protector, confidante, co-conspirator, partner-in-crime, soul mate, best friend, sounding board, greatest fan, personal chef, eternal lover ...' It's not enough for our spouse to care for us: they've got to champion us, challenge us, help us *grow*. We want them to awaken our sexual selves, expand our minds, hold our hand through 3am worries, inspire us to be the best we can be.

Modern marriages are creaking under the strain of these expectations. A friend who works as a couples' therapist tells me of the many times she has heard one partner complaining that their spouse is not 'growing' with them while the other partner looks utterly perplexed. Spool back to the early days of human pair-bonding and this level of expectation seems preposterous. Do you think Stone Age partners were berating each other about not letting them *grow*? Did they expect their partner and co-parent to telepathically understand their every need?

There is, quite simply, a huge gap between what human pair-bonding was designed for and what is expected of it today – and it's causing incalculable emotional fall-out in relationship break-down. The more expectations of marriage grow, the more likely it is to disappoint, the more resentful partners become, and the more they wonder what (or who) else is out there. This might explain why about 50 per cent of marriages now end in divorce, and why around one in five cheat – or admit to it, anyway.[1]

The romantic narrative that we absorb from our first Disney movie promises us – women *and* men – that love is poetry. When life delivers us prose, this causes heartache, disappointment and disastrous choices. The correction? Emulating the more pragmatic approach of our Stone Age past.

THE PALEO PRESCRIPTION
Ask less of love

A lot of the expectations piled on modern relationships come back to what I'd call the Grand Romantic Narrative. In an episode of 1950s-set drama *Mad Men*, advertising guru Don Draper is drinking with a woman who tells him that she has never been in love. Draper looks at her pitifully, 'What you call love ... was invented by guys like me to sell nylons.' The line is meant to expose his cynical heart, but is Draper so far from the truth? If we're talking about the modern idea of perfect, you-complete-me love, then fiction, advertising and the movies *do* have a lot to answer for.

From childhood we greedily consume the Grand Romantic Narrative: watching *Sleeping Beauty*; reading *Romeo and Juliet*, weeping through *The Notebook*. Women might be particularly targeted by 'chick flick' expectations but men are peddled the Grand Romantic Narrative too, learning from a young age that 'behind every great man is a great woman', and that success in life is nothing without success in love. In recent years men and women alike have swallowed some popular relationship notions: don't settle; hold out for the one; find someone who will still make your heart beat faster at ninety years old.

So in thrall are we to the Grand Romantic Narrative that it's no wonder our partners often fall short. They're our lover but not our friend, our friend but not our professional cheerleader, our cheerleader but not into croquet or obscure Korean films like we are. The gap between expectation and reality yawns wider. The modern answer to this dissatisfaction is to ask *more* of our partner and our relationship. The Stone Age answer? To ask *less*.

Spread the emotional load

Asking for less doesn't mean putting up with abuse, cruelty or neglect. It means getting some perspective on what one other person can and should provide you. At the beginning of my relationship there were certain things about my husband that frustrated me. When I was unwell he wasn't particularly attentive, not bringing me hot-water bottles like modern white knights are supposed to do. When I had a spasm of un-confidence about work projects he did little more than shrug his shoulders and say it would all turn out right in the end. When I wanted to share an amazing poem that I had read, he looked like he wanted to reach for a cyanide pill. If he cared, why couldn't he see I needed Lucozade, or a long pep talk? Why couldn't he try to enjoy what I enjoy?

I began noticing all the ways he was falling short. Steeped in women's magazine articles about how I should work out my 'needs' and get my partner to fulfil them, I initiated long debates. Communicate, communicate, communicate, goes the advice – and we did. But the same old arguments were had. I wanted my husband to share my priorities, read my feelings, anticipate what I needed. But the more I reflected on the prehis-toric roots of our relationship, the more I realised I was setting us up for failure.

I decided very consciously to take a load of expectation off the relationship – or rather to share the load. Yes, I need someone to commiserate with when I've had a hard day at work, someone to talk about my various symptoms with if I'm ill, someone to share some interesting article with – but who says they all have to be the same someone? Why not outsource some of the roles that (unfairly) a modern spouse is often expected to play? These days if I'm in need of a pep talk I will seek out my mother. If I want to speak for an hour about the highs and lows of motherhood, I'll call my friend Liz. If I want to get philosophical, I'll see Jules. If I want to watch an old Merchant Ivory film or reminisce on the beauties of Venice, I'll do that with my sister.

Spreading the emotional load like this has been called 'diversifying your social portfolio' – and it's strongly linked to wellbeing. Several studies have found that when someone has a range of different people to experience different emotions with, from sadness to triumph to reflectiveness, they have a higher quality of life.[2] Research like this is a riposte to the 'twin soul' idea that we've been fed by the Grand Romantic Narrative. My husband is still the central person I spend time with and talk to, but by not looking to him for everything I better appreciate all the good things that we share.

Beware romantic fantasies

Researchers from the University of Michigan surveyed 625 college students to see how their viewing habits influenced their beliefs about love. They found that more exposure to romantic movies led to a greater tendency to believe that 'love finds a way', whereas watching marriage-themed reality shows led participants to idealise 'true love'.[3] Another study found a direct link between the amount of romantic comedies people watched and the level of disappointment in their own marriage. Watching just one romcom such as *Notting Hill* was enough to sway people's attitudes to romantic love.[4]

I'm not suggesting that you don't ever watch or read anything with a romantic bent, but if your entertainment diet is romcoms plus a side helping of Mills & Boon, it's a good idea to view the messages in these stories through a more realistic lens. Remind yourself that 'perfect' relationships don't exist, that those heart-achingly lovely dialogues between on-screen lovers are dreamed up over coffee and doughnuts by a team of scriptwriters. It's not real — but its effect on your life could be.

Don't obsess about losing that lovin' feeling

Once upon a time your beloved might have walked miles through lashing rain just to see you, memorised all the players in the Premier League to impress you, named every freckle on your body with the reverence of Galileo naming the constellations ... Now they can barely tear their eyes from the telly when you talk about your day.

The fading of love's initial fire can be extremely painful. I should know: I sought therapy for it. I didn't get together with my husband until my mid-thirties, which meant that there was time for a few serious relationships before him – the kind of relationships in which you buy saucepans together and vaguely think that this might be 'it'. In each one I experienced a period of profound melancholy about eighteen months in, when it became clear that the first flush of attraction was fading. Falling from my pedestal as love object extraordinaire felt like a failing. After the third time this had happened, I sought the wisdom of a psychotherapist. 'Why does this keep happening? Why can't I have a relationship that lasts?'

Like countless others, I had bought into the idea – inspired by the Grand Romantic Narrative – that when the fizzy-and-obsessed phase is over, the whole relationship is over. It's what inspires people to declare those dreaded words 'I love you . . . but I'm not in love with you.' Behind these words is, again, a mismatch between modern expectation and age-old truth.

The modern expectation is that love should last with a burning intensity until death, or it ain't the real deal. But the age-old truth is that the first phase of love is not so much 'a total eclipse of the heart' as a total eclipse of the brain by feel-good chemicals – and those chemicals are time-limited.

Scientists suggest that the dopamine surge involved in early love fades somewhere between six months and two years into a relationship.[5] It doesn't matter if you're a Victoria's Secret model, a sexual athlete or the wittiest person alive, the reward pathway in your partner's brain won't keep firing the way it used to. Some may claim they still get goosebumps every day when their partner of thirty-odd years comes home but these are outliers. For most of us there comes an inevitable 'delirium drop-off' a couple of years in, when the dopamine subsides – and with it the giddy highs.

I find the inevitability of this reassuring. It's one reason why I stayed the course with my husband beyond those first couple of years. In previous relationships I felt the delirium drop-off so keenly that I would sabotage the relationship soon after. After all, if it felt like the partnership was nearing a natural end, why not pre-emptively show it the door? By the time I got together with my husband I knew better. I had reflected on how our species is hardwired to fall in lust and love. I was prepared not to freak out when things inevitably shifted after a couple of years.

The bottom line: experiencing the delirium drop-off doesn't mean you're 'falling out of love', as many people frame it. If tempted to seek that high elsewhere, remember that this is a stage that comes sooner or later to even the most all-conquering love. The fading of initial intensity isn't a failure or an ending but a natural part of a long-term relationship.

Make love a four-letter word

Telling someone 'I love you' for the first time is held up as one of life's climaxes. It's the crescendo in a song, the climax of a film, the moment readers crave for over two hundred pages of a romantic novel. But 'I love you' has become a lazy shortcut, a way of proving our feelings by mouthing a few words. As Agatha Christie once expressed, rather wearily: 'I am sick of words . . . "I love you! I love you!"; that parrot cry . . .'[6]

By the time I was thirty-five I had parroted 'I love you' to five men and whispered it mentally to a few more. Sometimes I meant it in the moment, sometimes I had felt compelled to say it (isn't it rude not to say 'I love you' back?), but frankly I was getting a little tired of it.

When I got together with my husband it was with a certain weariness that I realised we would soon be mouthing the ole I.L.Y.: the same words for a relationship that felt very different. As we had been friends for a long time I knew very quickly that I wanted only him for ever. I had always found him magnetic and magical. And now I would have to tether these very particular feelings to a very universal phrase: I love you.

Society decreed that we had to have the I.L.Y. moment. And yet we never did. Almost a decade and four children in, we have never said 'I love you' – and I love it. Because when you banish I.L.Y. from your relationship vocabulary, when you can't express your feelings in this easy way, you think harder about how you *show* them. With no I.L.Y. shortcut or sticking plaster you have to be more imaginative about how you bond, through actions and words.

Instead of I.L.Y. ...

- Tell them how they impress you: what do they do that often goes unnoticed? Where do you rely on their strengths to compensate for your weaknesses?
- Describe how they've made your life better.
- Compliment them in a way that you haven't done before.
- Don't say it, show it: use actions not words to demonstrate the strength of your feelings.

(Sometimes) it's good not to talk

Through the dark mists of time, here's one thing we can know about prehistoric couples: they were a practical team. The popular notion used to be of cave man the provider and cave woman the receiver: he'd throw a dead antelope on the floor; she'd cook it. But in recent years many have argued that this is way off the mark.

Both women and men had a role to play in the practical tasks that filled hunter-gatherers' lives: foraging, hunting, sharpening the spears, butchering the meat, fetching the water. One study suggests that women were probably superior hunters, with bodies better equipped for long-distance pursuit. Female skeletons show injuries consistent with being kicked by large animals, suggesting close contact with their prey. In short, researchers reckon that in prehistoric societies, no 'strict sexual division of labour existed'.[7] Working together on practical tasks with common goals was what underpinned their relationships.

You might think that modern couples are working on common goals together too: together we earn money, raise children, make sure the dishwasher is emptied. But so often the division of responsibilities in modern families leads to tension, not togetherness. In a family where both parents are working, men often feel that they're doing a lot by helping on the domestic front as well as earning money (which might be more than their father did), while women feel resentful because as well as earning they're doing more of the household chores. All this hardly induces the spirit of practical teamwork that underpinned prehistoric relationships.

That's why I believe it's important to have projects you work on together *outside* the necessary duties of earning a pay packet and sweeping the kitchen floor. I'm talking about hands-on, practical tasks that involve a couple being in the same space at the same time, problem-solving and being creative together. The small plot at the back of our house is no Garden of Eden but my husband and I have spent many contented hours discussing how we can improve it, planning features and researching plants, going to the garden centre and getting our hands into the soil. At Christmas time we like working out what outlandish displays we are going to create in our house. Every year I ask for the same thing for my birthday: something we can work on together, whether that's a piece of furniture to restore or a craft project to make.

My husband and I are at our best when working on something practical together, as our ancestors would have done every day – not when we are having deep 'n' meaningfuls. Modern relationship advice instructs us that communication is *everything*. We're encouraged to talk things out endlessly in the belief that this is the panacea to almost any problem in a relationship. But Professor John Gottman – a renowned expert on marriage – has found that 69 per cent of the problems among the couples he has studied are *never* resolved.[8] Sometimes the talking won't work. So then what? What I've found is that as we undertake practical tasks together, the old accusations and irritations recede. Instead of drained combatants facing each other having the same debates, you're collaborators working shoulder to shoulder. For millennia, human beings bonded as practical teams who had a job to do, not romantic partners who needed to complete each other. Sometimes it's not good to talk. It's better to do.

Stone Age wisdom on ... relationships

- We have been led to believe that we're destined for one true love that will complete us, conquer all obstacles, and fizz as fiercely in its fortieth year as in its first.
- Seeing partnership through a prehistoric lens helps to re-frame these unrealistic and unhelpful expectations.
- Our ancestors paired up for practical purposes, not to be 'completed'.
- Be sceptical about the Grand Romantic Narrative we have been fed, and be aware of the expectations it is creating around your own relationship.
- Be realistic about what one person can give you, diversifying your social portfolio so that your emotional needs are met by a range of people.
- Don't fret about falling out of love; the age-old hormones which produce that in-love euphoria have served their purpose after a year or two – and it's not a failure if those feelings fade.
- Instead of endlessly communicating about problems, try returning to the practical roots of partnership, undertaking hands-on tasks together.

11

Parenting and Children

A rainy day, lockdown, 2020. Months had been spent taking my young children (then aged two and one) to the same park, to play 'castles' on the same tree stump, to run around the same sad square of muddy grass. Then came a brainwave: pet shops were open, right? We could see real animals! Have a real outing! The possibility of seeing a guinea pig had me giddy. Half an hour later we were at the out-of-town pet superstore, which smelled enticingly of sawdust and hamster excrement. But, where were the animals? 'Yeah, they've all gone,' said the assistant. 'Covid.' Crushed, I dragged my children around the shop in search of anything interesting. And there it was, in the feed section. The only creatures left: a bowl of maggots. 'Look!' I cried. 'Look at that one! He's wiggling his tail in the air! Look at that little baby maggot, he's falling out of the bowl . . .' I looked at my nonplussed children and heard my desperate voice. The voice caught, a dam broke: I was weeping uncontrollably in the middle of the pet shop.

Sob after heaving sob, not only because of that botched

outing, but because the maggot meeting was a perfect encapsulation of all the boredom, loneliness and dashed expectations of motherhood. I had expected to be a magical mother, a turn-anything-into-fun mother, and most of all – since I had longed for babies for years – a happy mother.

But the truth was that I often wasn't happy, and felt terrible about it. I was extremely lonely, living in a new city a long way from family and friends. The eight or nine hours my husband was at work were a montage of windswept playgrounds and Norovirus-ridden soft plays set to the soundtrack of *In the Night Garden*, always just me and the babies, me and the babies. Yes, there were many moments of intense happiness: once, in a supermarket, I was smothering my daughter with kisses so passionately that someone joked we should 'get a room' – but the joy-to-boredom ratio wasn't great.

The worst of it was the guilt I felt: *Shouldn't I be enjoying this more?* My critical internal voice has always been a vicious little madam, and when it came to motherhood she was on fire: 'Some women aren't meant to be mothers, and you're one of them. Poor kids, having a mother like you.' So I fought my disappointment and tried desperately hard to enjoy those long, lonely days, but over them a question would hover: *Is motherhood really supposed to be like this?* Not according to the hunter-gatherers.

It takes a village

If you were to put a prehistoric mother in a time machine and drop her in 21st-century Chicago or Paris, one thing would shock her about modern-day parenting more than anything else. More than the buggies, sterilising equipment, and babies watching cartoons on iPads, she would be astounded by the sheer lack of support that most Western mothers have: the army of mothers on every high street pushing a buggy alone; the mothers frantically googling 'how to get baby to latch?' late at night, the mothers spending hours and hours alone with their child every day.

For hundreds of thousands of years, mothering was not something that mothers did largely alone. Anthropologist Sarah Blaffer Hrdy makes the argument that a long way back on our evolutionary journey – up to 1.8 million years ago – mothers among our hominid ancestors began to embrace collective parenting, passing their babies into others' arms. Gradually, the raising of children began to be shared by a network of grandmothers, aunts, uncles, siblings and friends, collectively known as 'alloparents' ('allo' is derived from 'other').[1]

'Without alloparents,' Hrdy writes, 'there never would have been a human species.' Why? Because raising human beings from infancy to independence is a monumental task. Human babies are incredibly slow to mature: unable to walk at birth, unable to protect themselves for many years. Raising them requires a huge amount of energy to be expended on feeding, carrying and tending to their needs. It needs constant vigilance, at least in the early years. Therefore, for mothers to be able to be successful in the evolutionary sense – for them to rear their child to adulthood *and* have more children – they needed plenty of helping hands.

Several studies back up Hrdy's theory, finding that where child mortality rates are high (as they were in prehistoric times), the presence of alloparents is crucial to children's survival. In 2000 the anthropologist Paula Ivey discovered that among the Efé (who live in the rainforest of the Democratic Republic of Congo), the number of alloparents a baby had at age one was correlated with how likely the child was to be alive at three.[2] Another study looked at data taken from the Mandinka horticulturalists in the Gambia between 1950 and 1980, and found something extraordinary: if a child had older siblings and a maternal grandmother living locally, the chance of them dying before the age of five was halved.[3]

The saying that 'it takes a village to raise a child' was meant literally for most of human existence. In traditional societies around the world, alloparenting is still the way people raise their young. By the time an Efé baby is a week or so old, they have experienced care from an average of 14 alloparents.[4] Some of these caregivers bond with babies by kiss-feeding, in which saliva sweetened with honey or other foods is passed from the mouth of the adult to the mouth of the infant. Although this might raise Western eyebrows, it shows how close the alloparent–child relationship can be.

Of course we are exhausted

Learning about alloparenting was a game-changing moment for me, re-framing motherhood and my own 'failures'. For the first two years of parenting I had felt I was failing at something that couldn't be more natural. If I was meant to be Velcroed to my baby 24/7 like a chimpanzee mother, why did I find it exceptionally hard and draining?

But no mother is *meant* to be doing this gargantuan job largely alone. The idea of the nuclear family – and its connected ideal of the do-it-all mother – is a recent construct in human history. Just 150 years or so ago it was the norm, even in Western societies, for mothers to be well supported: the rich and reasonably off had nannies and cooks, the poor had large extended families, with teenage cousins or older siblings on hand to help. A 2023 study by Cambridge University anthropologists emphasises that alloparenting is a core human adaptation, and warns that the 'intensive mothering' narratives that hold sway in much of the West 'can lead to maternal exhaustion and have dangerous consequences'.[5]

For all those mothers and fathers who beat themselves up for finding this 'natural' part of life so inexplicably hard, remember that it isn't natural to do the work that several people used to do. It isn't natural for parents to pass the baton of childcare between them without a wider support network. It isn't natural for new mothers to head home two days after giving birth to start navigating breastfeeding, sleeping and raising a tiny human without a slew of aunties and cousins to help them. In the context of all humankind, the way we parent today in the West is an aberration. As historian John R. Gillis put it: 'Never have mothers been so burdened by motherhood.'[6]

Of course, many in the West are lucky enough to have alloparents nearby: they live near grandparents or siblings, or they have a tight circle of friends who mind each other's children. But those who don't have that support – and who find parenthood brutal – should re-frame their struggle. In the context of human history, parenting in a nuclear family is an extraordinary achievement, so give yourself a huge break for any of your perceived 'failings'. In fact, give yourself a round of applause. You're not just doing what parents have done for millennia, you're doing *more*.

A different way

As someone who has long been fascinated by hunter-gatherers, it seems odd, in retrospect, that for my first couple of years as a parent I didn't bother to explore how they parent. I assumed, in that arrogant Western way, that we had the business of child rearing cracked. Weren't there NHS websites and health visitors to tell me what to do? How hard could it be?

I set to work with schedules and sleep training, strict rules and a determination that through iron will I would mould perfectly behaved, obedient little children. While pregnant with my first I recall telling a friend (only half-jokingly) that my child would be raised 'in a benign dictatorship', with boundaries from day one.

A couple of years in, I started to hear a tone in my own voice that I didn't like: shouting, scolding, saying 'Don't!' thirty-eight times before breakfast. I loathed this voice – and so did my oldest daughter. After one killer tantrum, she (then two years old) finished with a killer line: 'Want another mummy.' Ouch! OK, I thought. I'll give you another mummy. I'll change. Thus began my exploration of hunter-gatherer parenting, which surprised, provoked and inspired me.

A couple of disclaimers. First, I don't intend to romanticise the experience of parenting in hunter-gatherer bands, for the simple reason that the children in these societies were – and are – far more likely than children in modern industrialised nations to die before they had reached adulthood. One study that looked at seventeen Paleolithic and modern hunter-gatherer societies found that 49 per cent of children died. What untold agony lies behind this figure.

Second, talking about a 'hunter-gatherer approach' to parenting is as broad brush as a 'Western approach' to parenting. Different societies have different ways of supporting mothers, nurturing babies, disciplining children, instilling them with values, and so on. But across hunter-gatherer societies – and those which also rely on agriculture but which we might term 'traditional' societies – there are recurring features in the way that they parent their children:

Feature 1: alloparenting

The village raises the child. From a young age it is perfectly normal for non-parents to feed, comfort and play with a baby. Just an hour or two after being born, newborns in the Aka tribe are handed around the campfire to be kissed and comforted by their new alloparents. In the months to come they will be passed between these caregivers about eight times per hour (yes, an anthropologist was there to count every squeeze and cuddle).[7]

Feature 2: attentiveness

The notion that responding to what a baby wants is spoiling them or 'creating a rod for your own back' is anathema in hunter-gatherer societies, where a child's cries tend to be responded to instantly. A wailing Efé infant can expect a response within about ten seconds. For !Kung babies, 88 per cent of crying bouts receive a response of cuddling or feeding within three seconds.[8]

Feature 3: closeness

Whereas babies in developed societies spend large chunks of time in their playpen or bouncy chair, hunter-gatherers' babies are cuddled and carried around the clock. During the day !Kung infants spend their first year of life in skin-to-skin contact with the mother or another caregiver for 90 per cent of the time.[9] At night, babies and children sleep next to their mother.

Feature 4: freedom

Whereas anxious Western parents helicopter over their young with wet wipes and plasters, hunter-gatherers stand back. Among the Mbendjele BaYaka Pygmies of the Congo rainforest, toddlers carry machetes.[10] In the New Guinea Highlands, children are allowed to play with fire.[11] Packs of children of all ages go off and roam together, out of adult sight for hours – much like Western children did until the 1970s. This level of freedom might make us wince, but for many hunter-gatherers raising your children properly means granting them real – and risky – autonomy.

Feature 5: child-inclusive, not child-centred

In the Rouffignac Caves of Dordogne, France is a glimpse of Stone Age childhood. High on the walls are several small finger flutings: long lines made by fingers combed through the clay. The artists: children as young as three. Remarkably, archaeologists can tell that the most prolific young finger-fluter was a girl of about five.[12] We can picture her now, sitting on her father's shoulders, delighting in the cool, damp feeling under her fingers.

In cave art around the world we see the work of mini-artists. The inclusion of children in this important (and perhaps sacred) task suggests that the worlds of adults and children weren't separate ones. The play of children was woven into the adult world. Tiny spear flints and other mini tools found from Sweden to Jordan suggest that then – as now – children loved playing at being grown-up. In hunter-gatherer societies today children's main activities are shadowing and imitating the grown-ups. They emulate hunting, build mini straw huts, dig for tubers alongside their mothers and grandmothers. With no mountains of brightly coloured plastic toys to entertain them, their play is to explore the adult world.

Babies passed between loving adults; toddlers taking the hand of their older siblings or cousins; easy affection between alloparents and children; little ones exploring the world unbound by too many rules; the trend of unhurried quantity time over manic quality time: if there is a thread running through all this, it is grace. While parenting in the West is so often fraught, anxious, neurotic and schedule-obsessed, parenting in traditional communities seems admirably unhurried, calm, *graceful*. It's this grace that I try to infuse into the way I parent. Often failing, yes, but I try.

THE PALEO PRESCRIPTION
Parent with grace

Let's start with some realism. It is hardly possible (or desirable) to emulate everything hunter-gatherer parents did, or do today. If we live in a city where the temperature is below freezing for months on end, round-the-clock skin-to-skin is not going to happen. If we were to let our kids play with knives, social services might have something to say about it. If we are raising our children to be adults in the Western world, they have to learn the rules of the Western world. But there *are* overall lessons to be drawn from a way of life – and parenting – that our species practised for hundreds of thousands of years. Here are the key lessons I've taken for my own life.

Seek community

The most clear and important lesson from hunter-gatherer parenting is to seek or build a community in which to raise your child. This might be easier said than done. These days we often end up far from our original home town, settling wherever fate, fortune or love has taken us. It's become perfectly normal to live hours from family and close friends. But here's the hunter-gatherer-inspired advice for the far flung: if relocating to live near family is at all an option, seriously consider it. For some people, moving back to their home town might feel like a retrograde step. We've got it into our heads that we should leave the nest at eighteen and make our own way. But the fundamental importance of having that wider family network around should never be underestimated.

Still, living close to family isn't an option for all of us, including me, so I've had to build my own alloparenting network. As an introvert, this doesn't come naturally. But I forced myself to attend the circuit of toddler groups, banging tambourines to 'The Wheels on the Bus' and scanning the room for possible allies.

Learning about alloparenting has also transformed how I think about getting help with raising my children. I used to think that mothers who got help – in or outside the home – were self-indulgent and pampered. Why couldn't they just crack on with it like mothers had since the dawn of time? But as we've established, mothers *haven't* done it alone. If the support network isn't there, feel no shame about getting help if you can afford it.

The bottom line: we are not meant to do this alone. Seek community. Move closer to family if you can. Make friends. Build your circle. And, if possible, get help.

Learn to submit

For me, one word has unlocked an easier way of parenting. That word is 'submission'. Learning to submit is an instant mental trick that makes parenting eight times easier. Let's clarify. Talk of being a submissive parent and people imagine brats running amok while right-on parents pontificate about the need to allow their children to express themselves. I'm not talking about submitting to your kids' every whim, but submitting to the *reality* of parenthood.

The reality is that raising children is often chaotic, complicated, unpredictable – and so much of Western parenting seems to fight this reality. We want a child to sit neatly in the child-shaped hole in our lives, to follow schedules and do as we expect them to do. We want them to be a pleasant addition to our life rather than an energy-sucking transformer of it. We want to control the situation, and to control them.

This bid for control starts in early babyhood. By the time my first baby was a couple of months old I had been advised to feed her strictly at 7am, 10am, 2pm, 5pm, 7pm and 11pm. I had been told that she had to sleep at all times in her cot, and that letting her nap on me would be something I would regret. When, at four months, she wouldn't be put down, I was told that she was learning she could get her way; if she cried until I picked her up again, she was calling the shots (which wasn't good).

And so motherhood was established as a battle of wills. I had to lay down rules and boundaries and show the baby who was boss, or risk raising a spoiled terror who would be the living embodiment of my failed parenting. The schedules and rules were meant to help but, looking back, all the most miserable moments in those early years happened when I had tried and failed to control a situation: when a baby woke early from a nap that was meant to last two hours precisely; when a nine-month-old was refusing to eat anything but baby rice when the books said she needed protein at lunch; when baby would not go to sleep unless I stroked her hair for twenty minutes, when she was meant to be 'self-settling'. Having so many expectations and rules meant that I was constantly 'failing'. I couldn't control the situation, causing frequent anxiety.

Learning about hunter-gatherer parenting sparked a realisation. Maybe, like parents for millennia before me, I should just ... submit. Not fret about exact nap times or feeding times. Not worry if they weren't doing ten minutes of tummy time or if they only had a hot cross bun for lunch. My internal mantra: 'So what?' The baby doesn't want a bath for a couple of nights in a row: 'So what?' Baby has two naps instead of one: 'So what?' Submitting to the realities of parenthood transformed the experience of having my third baby. I kept my expectations of how a day would unfold low and loose. She slept when she slept, fed when she fed. Instead of desperately doing front crawl against the current, I started going with the flow – and the relief was immense.

Stay close

Most importantly, I've submitted to my children's desire for closeness. In the 1950s and 1960s the psychologist Harry Harlow conducted a series of controversial experiments on newborn rhesus monkeys.[13] Separating them from their mothers imme-diately after birth, he placed them in cages with access to two surrogate mothers. 'Mother' 1 was made of wire, but attached to her was a baby bottle containing milk. 'Mother' 2 was made of soft terry towelling cloth. Which did the baby monkeys prefer? When hungry they would drink milk from the wire mother. But the rest of the time, they only wanted the soft terry-cloth mother. When a frightening object was placed in the cage, they took refuge with the cloth mother. They slept with 'her', too. Harlow's explanation: infants have an innate need for touch, a desire as strong – or stronger – than hunger.

While traditional societies understand this need, in develop-ing societies we have partially forgotten it. Yes, we encourage skin-to-skin in the early weeks, but beyond that we expect a baby or toddler to spend most of their time separate from us: in a pram, a bouncer, a high chair. Carrying them too much is even seen by some as an indulgence. Since my baby son would scream and arch his back whenever he was put in a bouncing chair, he spent his first eighteen months on my hip, a sight which would inevitably make my mother roll her eyes and mutter about how he 'needed to learn'.

Look, we can't carry babies all the time. For people with more than one child, or a bad back, or other commitments, it's not realistic. Toddlers get heavy – and many people don't have allo-parents to (literally) share the load. But the basic point is this: forget about the notion that by responding to a child and cud-dling them day or night, you are 'spoiling' them. The experience of millennia would suggest this is nonsense.

> **Tips for closeness**
>
> - Where possible, opt to carry baby in a sling rather than push them in a buggy.
> - Have day-time reading sessions in bed with babies or toddlers, cuddling in a nest of pillows to read.
> - If you can bear a few peas on the floor, let toddlers eat sitting on your lap, not always in the high chair.
> - If they are walking, get down to their level regularly, floor sitting and lap sitting.
> - Try playing without toys and props – rolling around on the floor, enjoying physical play.

The co-sleeping taboo

It was quiet in the hospital on the day our first child was born, so we were given our own room. In it was a bed for me and a little wooden cot for baby. After cuddling and feeding her, I put my newborn down in the cot, said goodnight and expected her to drop off into her first sleep (she didn't, of course).

Of all the things I have done as a parent this seems the most absurd. Our tiny girl, who had been warm in my womb for nine months, was left rolling around on cool cotton bed sheets. Why? Because we in the West are instructed that there is only one way we should let our children sleep, which is separate from us. They are to sleep for their first year in a cot in the same room as their parents, and thereafter in a room on their own.

The entirely understandable fear of cot death has given us a fear of sharing a bed with a baby. I get it. I shared it. With my first baby I followed the guidelines on safe sleeping for months. By 4am she would be sleeping on me and I would be wide awake, terrified that I was about to squash and kill her. Those were not halcyon days for my mental health. Eventually, the odd cuddle to get my daughter back to sleep turned into whole nights in the same bed, which turned into a way of life (or way of sleeping). Our four children – now six, four, three and six months – still spend some or all of the night in bed with one or both of us.

Mention that you co-sleep in this day and age, and you are at risk of looking like a weirdo. So accustomed are we to separate sleeping that co-sleeping seems odd and unnatural – not to mention disastrous for the parental relationship. I accept that co-sleeping might not be the secret to marital bliss for many. It can be maddening sleeping with a child kicking you every four seconds, or having to creep out to the toilet because you don't want to wake a slumbering toddler. But it can also be exceptionally *nice*. Hearing my children's breathing, feeling their warm forms next to me; these have been some of the best moments of mothering. To me it feels entirely natural, probably because in the long span of human life this *was* entirely natural.

Throughout the Stone Age our ancestors slept next to their children, not just because this was pleasant and warm for all parties but also because leaving a baby to sleep in the wild among vicious predators would have been a dumb thing to do. As author and paediatrician Carlos González puts it, 'Mothers who left their children alone for more than a few minutes soon had no children. Their genes were eliminated by natural selection. By contrast, the genes that compelled mothers to stay with their children were passed down to numerous descendants. You are one of those descendants.'[14]

I am no evangelist for co-sleeping: what works for some doesn't for others. If it's going to wreck your mental health and prevent you from functioning, I wouldn't do it. But don't be put off by thinking it's unnatural to sleep alongside your child, because that couldn't be further from the truth.

How to co-sleep safely

- Avoid co-sleeping with babies under eighteen months if you are a heavy sleeper.
- Babies or children should never share a bed with someone who smokes or who has been drinking heavily.
- With young babies it's safer to sleep with one parent rather than two.
- If sleeping with babies (as opposed to toddlers), never use pillows or thick covers on the bed; instead use light sheets and breathable blankets that only reach up to their stomach.

- Don't co-sleep on memory mattresses or anything too squashy; the bed should be reasonably firm.
- Ensure that a baby is not sleeping near a gap between the bed and the wall, down which they could get stuck.
- Never co-sleep with a baby on a sofa.
- Keep the temperature in the room cool: 16–20 degrees centigrade.
- For more advice on safe co-sleeping, see lullabytrust. org.uk.

Mini-me parenting

At the back of my childhood garden were some four-foot-high weeds: a mini-forest in which I could hide and entertain myself for hours with just a doll for company. Was I bored? Probably, sometimes, but from that boredom flowered imagination, creating stories from the stuff of weeds and ants and broken wheelbarrows. So much of the magic of childhood happens in those 'boring' stretches of time when nothing much is created. And yet initially, I denied my children the possibility of feeling bored, or of inventing their own play at all.

I wanted everything to be fun, which meant daily itineraries of soft plays, zoos, petting farms and cinema trips. Every minute was maxed out for kiddie enjoyment, with nursery rhymes playing in the car, coloured bubbles in the bath and play dough on tap. Every day, from the age of six months, my daughter would go to at least one activity, often two: swimming class, 'messy play', singing group, baby gym, toddler football, mini disco dancing. I spent hundreds on bubble wands and pipe cleaners so that there would never be a dull moment. Once, when rummaging through my bag for something, my husband pulled out some thin balloons I had shaped into a dog. 'Who are you, Crusty the Clown?'

I was trying too hard, which we Western parents tend to do. We obsess about having quality time with our children, treating them like VIPs who need to be catered to. In contrast, hunter-gatherers enjoy relaxed *quantity* time in which their children are simply included in adult activities, or left to play and emulate what the grown-ups are doing. While Western parenting is child-centred, hunter-gatherer parenting might more accurately be described as child-inclusive.

It's an approach I try to follow. I call it mini-me parenting. Instead of filling up our days with child-focused activities (which, frankly, can be soul-destroyingly dull), we find activities that we can all do together. This often means household chores: gardening, shopping, cooking, laundry. At cleaning time my children have little water-filled spray bottles and cloths to wipe down cupboards. In the garden they water plants and pull up weeds. Ten minutes might be happily spent pairing up a bag of odd socks. My son loves to vacuum clean. While this may sound a little like unpaid child labour, they love it.

This doesn't mean that we never go to soft play; we are just much more relaxed about allowing them to play in an organic way. Instead of acting like obsequious concierges trying to keep our VIPs endlessly entertained, we treat them where possible as collaborators.

Mini-me activities

For one- to two-year-olds

- 'Sorting out' the receipts, credit cards and money in your purse (watch for choking hazards like coins)
- Washing up at the sink
- Wiping the table clean

For three- to four-year-olds

- Window cleaning with a bucket of soapy water and rags
- Making sandwiches
- Mopping the floor

For five- to ten-year-olds

- Baking a cake
- Gardening
- Watering the plants

Be a guide, not a controller

I'm never going to be a parent who lets their kid play with fire or wander off on their own for hours. Here my willingness to walk the hunter-gatherer path ends. Yet I do admire the space that parents in traditional societies tend to give their young. Their children are allowed to explore without constant hectoring and controlling. As far as I can, I've curbed my instinct to endlessly screech *'Stop!' 'Come here!' 'Don't do that!'*

Instead of telling them *not* to do things I want to gently nudge them in a safer or better direction. But how, when the words 'don't' and 'no' sit so naturally on the tip of my tongue? As someone who responds well to clear rules, I realised that the only way I could discipline myself enough to change was to reclassify these as swear words. Yes, in my book 'no' and 'don't' are the new 'b******s' and 's**t'. This may sound strange, but thinking of these words as taboo helps to filter my responses. In the same way that some people substitute four-letter words for ones like 'fudge', I'm now in the habit of swapping out negative warnings for positive exhortations. Instead of 'be careful!' I say: 'can you show me how well you can get down?'

No-proof your home

If your children are living in an environment where there is lots to break, ruin or create havoc with, you're setting them up to fail – and setting yourself up to endlessly shout '*No!*' Why not create a space where exploration is less fraught?

- If you have crawling babies or infants, use stair gates to close off the areas where they shouldn't be going.
- Switch out glassware and china plates for plastic alternatives.
- Keep knives in a high, locked box – likewise all other dangerous objects and chemicals.
- Cover sharp corners on furniture.
- Use furniture covered with easily washable slip covers or made of leather.
- Have drawers at their height full of old utensils and junk-shop finds to play with.
- Secure large objects such as chests of drawers and wardrobes to the wall to make them climb-friendly.
- Paint walls with washable, child-proof paint.

Stone Age wisdom on . . . parenting

- Involve other adults where possible; building a 'village' to help raise children.
- Submit to the messy realities of parenting, whether they fit the Western mould or not.
- Prioritise physical closeness: cuddling, carrying, contact – perhaps even co-sleeping.

- Instead of endlessly catering to children's desires, incorporate their play into the rhythms of your life.
- Give them more freedom: curbing the desire to correct them all the time, creating an environment where they can explore without regularly being told 'no'.

12

Town and Country

Cities mean glamour and glory, fame and fortune, vigour and vim: Paris in the springtime, the neon lights of Tokyo, Holly Golightly trotting down Fifth Avenue. Cities are where we go to 'make it'; to be inspired, connected, thrilled.

In my twenties I blew the budget on renting a matchbox-sized apartment on Charlotte Street in the very centre of London. I was in the belly of the beast – and I loved it. The night's lullaby was the far-off wail of sirens, the dawn chorus the judder of refuse trucks. With a dozen restaurants just doors away, the air was thick with garlic or turmeric depending on the way the wind was blowing. As I trotted down to work, grabbing a bagel on the way and weaving deftly through hundreds of strangers, I felt the epitome of a City Girl. But when serious anxiety hit me, a strange thing happened. The city turned on me. The vibrancy became exhausting, the smells suffocating, the endless parade of faces overwhelming. On the worst days – when all 600 muscles in my body were simultaneously clenched – I would walk down to the Thames and turn east, marching for two, three, four hours straight until the city began to thin out. True, my yearning for space would have been better served by jumping on a train to the countryside, but somehow I wanted to regain control over my environment, to feel the city dissolve beneath my pacing feet.

By the outer reaches of London I could breathe again. With the crowded heart of the city far behind me, and a broader, less cluttered sky ahead, my ribcage would finally expand. In those moments of reflection, gazing down at the broad, brown Thames, a vague but important-feeling thought took shape: something about the city was disagreeing with something deep in my core.

The rural-to-urban switch

City living is a blink in the eye of the human story. It wasn't until 2007 that more people lived in cities than in rural areas.[1] Just three hundred years ago almost 95 per cent of us lived in rural, low-density areas.[2] No one at all lived in a city until about 7000 BCE, when Çatalhüyük was settled in what is now Turkey. For the two million-odd years that humans had walked the earth before that, we lived in forest and jungle, on plain and savannah.

Our species may be good at adapting, but has the switch from rural to urban living happened too quickly for us to adapt to? Data which links city living to mental-health problems certainly raises the question. Urbanites' likelihood of suffering generalised anxiety disorder is 21 per cent higher than rural dwellers.[3] The risk of developing depression is 20 per cent higher and psychosis a startling 77 per cent higher.[4] The incidence of schizophrenia is twice as high in those born and raised in cities.[5] Can differences this stark be explained only by the higher rates of poverty and inequality often found in cities? Or are they also explained by the stress that comes from living in habitats our brains haven't evolved to cope with?

We might think that being subjected to constant noise, sights and strangers is a natural part of life, but our amygdala – the 'fight or flight' part of our brain – begs to differ. Researchers from the University of Heidelberg asked fifty city dwellers and country folk to perform stressful tasks while their brains were being scanned. Were the hardened city types more immune to stress? Far from it. In fact, the urbanites' amygdala was over-active when placed under stress. City-induced stress was actually *causing* abnormalities in key areas of the brain, leading in turn to increased mental-health problems.[6]

Shocks to the Stone Age system

What exactly about city life is so stressful that it can alter the way parts of our brain function? If we were to scoop up an early human and drop them into modern-day Tokyo or Buenos Aires, the first shock to hit them would be the sheer number of people. For over 99 per cent of our history we humans lived in bands of thirty to fifty people who were not only our family and friends but also our ticket to survival.

Imagine, then, how wary you might have been of a stranger

entering the group. Not knowing whether this person meant good or ill, you wouldn't be able to relax fully around them for a while. The effort involved in figuring new people out is a kind of stress – which might partly explain why increasing population density has been linked to increasing mental-health problems. One study, conducted in Sweden, found that as the number of people per square kilometre climbs, so too do rates of depression.[7] Another looked at high-density cities in Brazil, which were associated with a 21 per cent higher likelihood of elevated depressive symptoms among women and a 21 per cent higher likelihood of suicidal thoughts among men, regardless of income.[8] Is this our prehistoric brains suffering the shock of too many people?

Another jolt to the Stone Age system is urban noise. We evolved to be acutely sensitive to sound. For hundreds of thousands of years, hearing was an essential tool for staying alive – and for some it still is. Anthropologist Jerome Lewis describes a hunting trip through dense forest with the Mbendjele people of Congo-Brazzaville: 'All members of the party, children included, react instantly to a crack, a low rumble, or an animal call by stopping mid-step, balancing on one leg if necessary. Silent and motionless, they strain to hear any follow-up sounds that will tell them to run for their lives, chase after supper, or just continue onwards.'[9]

These things on the sides of our head have evolved to be exquisitely sensitive. Now think about how stressful it is to expose them to the cacophony of the average city: shouts, car horns, music blaring. Noise pollution affects our blood biochemistry even more than exhaust fumes do.[10] It is linked to type-2 diabetes.[11] It triggers the release of the stress hormone cortisol, damaging blood vessels and leading to high blood pressure and heart attacks.[12] People living next to noisy roads are 25 per cent more likely to have symptoms of depression, regardless of their financial situation or background.[13] Because we are acclimatised to constant intrusive noise we have come to think of this as natural, but in the long span of human life it really isn't.

Square world vs round world

Perhaps the greatest shock for our Stone Age time traveller would not be the people or the noise but – aside from the odd park – the lack of nature. While living in London and suffering severe anxiety I managed to haul myself to a nearby café to meet a friend, an elderly Greek gentleman who was my go-to Wise Man. I told him about my anxiety: the feeling that the city itself was strangling me. He slowly chewed a piece of croissant, staring into space, before declaring in his delightfully thick accent: 'Your problem is this: you spend too much time in the square world and not enough time in the round world.' Come again?

'You sit in a flat which is square and watch a television which is square. You walk on roads which are straight into buildings which are square. You look at computers all day which are square. Too many straight lines. It is hurting your soul. Your soul was meant to be in the round world.'

While the square world–round world concept seemed mad at the time, in recent years I have come to see the wisdom in it.

Take a look at the diagram below. You may have seen it before, but play along: which line is longer?

The Muller-Lyer illusion

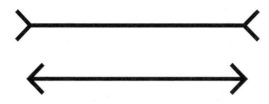

The line on top might look longer, but they're the same length. Scientists used to believe that all humans' vision was wired to perceive such things in the same way. Then, in the 1960s, anthropologists presented this same illusion to members of the Zulu tribe in South Africa. They didn't fall for the trick. Why? Because, the researchers argued, they had spent their lives in nature, where straight lines and corners are extremely uncommon. In contrast, we in the industrialised West grow up in an environment full of straight lines, boxy buildings and carpeted corners. That means that when we see these lines, our brains leap to perceive the arrows on their ends as the corners of rooms or buildings, which in turn skews our perception of their length.

Although you may be wondering what on earth this has to do with cities and nature, the different way we see the Muller-Lyer illusion reveals something fascinating. The environment we grow up in isn't a passive backdrop which has little effect on us: it shapes the way we perceive things and even how our brains function. For most of our time on this earth we lived in the world of curved lines and uneven, organic shapes – the 'round world' that my Greek friend described, with no straight lines aside from the distant horizon. Now we live for most of the time in the 'square world', surrounded by straight lines, boxes and corners. Could this, at some deep level, be affecting our Stone Age equilibrium? Our yearning for nature would suggest so.

An evolutionary need for nature

In the 1930s a little boy named Edward O. Wilson was fishing in a river near his Alabama home when the edge of a catch he was reeling in blinded him in one eye. The accident was to change the course of his life. Unable to see too well out of the other eye either, he became preoccupied with watching tiny creatures like ants, a hobby that inspired a stellar career. Wilson became a famed Harvard biologist who proposed many interesting theories, among them 'biophilia': 'the innately emotional affiliation of human beings to other living organisms'.[14] Wilson's argument was that because humans have co-evolved with nature, we need daily contact with it.

Although it's easy to dismiss biophilia as a tree-huggy notion, a growing body of evidence would suggest that humans do *need* nature. Spending time in nature has been found to lower stress, decrease blood pressure and reduce anxiety. It helps to protect us from respiratory diseases.[15] It boosts our immune system.[16] It has even been linked to lower levels of crime.[17] Hospital patients who enjoy window views that are bright and green recover faster than those with no windows, or who look out on to man-made environments.[18]

Natural light is particularly important, a proven booster of productivity, mood and sleep. Our ancestors reaped these benefits because they spent the majority of time outside. Meanwhile, those living in the industrialised world now spend up to 90 per cent of their time indoors.[19]

When you look at the evidence, the idea that humans *need* nature seems less like hippy theory and more like fact. We evolved in close proximity to nature, yet for many people today their nature 'fix' is a birdsong noise on their sleep app or a waterfall on their screensaver. It's not enough.

THE PALEO PRESCRIPTION
Go where the wild things are

Satisfying our biophilia means spending a good amount of time outdoors. Every. Single. Day. To some this will seem impossible. Where's the time? We have jobs, families, chores, and so on. But I've come to realise that exposure to nature is so essential to wellbeing that the space for it *has* to be carved out. That means re-framing nature not as a luxury but as a necessity. Would you skip meals for days because you don't have time? Would you stop bathing for a week because you don't have time? Would you forget to sleep because you don't have time? 'Don't have time' shouldn't be a reason to avoid that other life essential: nature.

I get out twice every day, morning and afternoon. It's such a long-term habit that if I fail to make it out twice I feel like a stir-crazy dog that needs walking. It wasn't always easy to do, as I used to hate being in the cold, and I live in the northern hemisphere. It's easy to get out in nature when it's 20 degrees Celsius and the skies are turquoise, harder when they are ominously grey. But our bodies need light and nature all year round, so I had to make peace with the seasons.

To do that you've got to have the right clothing. This might sound trivial, but it's essential to a nature-rich life. Observe the average Briton in winter and you will see that often they're wearing one layer too little. No coat in a storm, shorts when it's minus weather. I didn't realise how foolish this was until I spent some time in Sweden in the middle of winter. I was woefully unprepared, dressed in a thin coat in temperatures of minus two.

A friend there shared a Swedish expression: there's no such thing as bad weather, only bad clothes. Inspired, I bought a Swedish-made winter coat, which could withstand a polar expedition. This coat is ugly as sin, as my husband frequently reminds me, but it is also a duvet with sleeves. It means the great outdoors is open to me all year round. It means that into late autumn I can eat outside at our patio table. In short, the right clothes are the difference between embracing nature, or not.

Forests: nature's pharmacy

Forests are my natural anti-depressant and favourite habitat.

'Go to the woods and hills! No tears | Dim the sweet look that Nature wears ...' as Longfellow put it.[20] Being in a creaking, sighing, breathing forest is nature on steroids, and science suggests it is powerfully good for us. The Japanese practice of *shinrin-yoku* – or forest bathing – has been found to improve mood, lower blood pressure, decrease cortisol levels and boost the immune system.[21] These profound benefits mean that forest bathing experiences are offered all over the world, many of them free. If you'd rather forest bathe alone or with a friend than in a group, here are the basics.

- Carve out a couple of hours to be in the forest; don't book-end it with deadlines.
- Dress well for the weather.
- Turn off your devices or leave them at home.
- Deliberately slow your pace; you are there to meander and observe, not to reach a destination.
- Slow your breathing – breathe in for four seconds, hold for seven, exhale for eight.
- Commit your senses to your surroundings. If you close your eyes, can you isolate different birds' songs? What do the different trees feel like? What can you smell?
- Look up at the branches of the trees, allow them to become an abstract picture against the sky.

- Find a place to sit and observe all the details in the scene around you.
- Don't think that you have to enter some transcendental state for this to be effective; it's observing while wandering.
- Although a couple of hours is a good stretch for forest bathing, don't stretch it out if you've had enough. The forest will wait for the next time.

How to build nature into your life

Rethink it Frame daily exposure to nature as both a treat and a necessity, not a chore. Remember that our ancestors were outside all day, every day. Regardless of the weather, this is what we were built for. Nurture yourself.

Schedule it If you live in the city, you're not just going to suddenly find yourself in nature, so it's a good idea to schedule it in. Could you leave for work earlier and make a pit stop somewhere green on your way? Is there a park you can visit during your lunch break? In the summer when it's light until late, could you head to your nearest lake instead of switching on the TV?

List it Because the same old green space can get boring, draw up a list of at least ten different places that you could get to easily enough – even if they're a short bus or car trip away. City dwellers might think this difficult, but there are likely to be acres of green space not too far from you. There are over 3,000 parks in London, 400 in Bristol, 150 in Manchester. New York City contains 20,000 acres of nature. It's probably there if you go looking for it.

Resolve to do it The lure of the screen or sofa can be so strong that it is helpful to make some clear resolutions about getting into nature. One of my resolutions is that once a year I sleep under the stars. How about thinking of your own resolutions? Such as: once a day, I'll go outside for at least half an hour with no digital distractions; once a week, I'll go on a two-hour-long walk; once a month, I will go for a day trip to a natural attraction that I've never been to before, such as a woodland, a river, a garden.

Seek respite from the city

Although cities can be energising, for those who live or work in one, it's wise to recognise that our Stone Age brains sometimes need respite from busy, crowded, noisy places. For me, in practical terms, that means:

Seeking city sanctuaries While working in Westminster I held a mental map of all the places within about a mile's walk of my office that promised space, quiet and distance from the madding crowd. If I felt my shoulders tensing up towards my earlobes I would head to one of them for respite. My favourite was Westminster Cathedral, its vast ceilings swallowing all noise and swiftly bestowing calm on all who enter. Whether you are in downtown Lagos or Los Angeles, there are likely to be sanctuaries not too far from you: public libraries, churches and garden squares normally deliver.

Tuning out the noise Even if we don't feel bothered by the 60-decibel assault on our ears, science suggests that our bodies certainly are. Although not a gadget person, I have found noise-cancelling headphones make a real difference when I'm forced into the heart of the city, or the airport, or anywhere else where loud noises jangle my Stone Age nerves. These can be very expensive, but the ones I picked up for around £50 work well enough.

Making home a sanctuary My wise friend warned me about the wearying effects of living in the 'square world', so I try to make my home as 'round world' as possible, looking for furniture and objects that reflect the curves and organic shapes of nature. And – of course – I love having lots of houseplants around the place. The thicker the indoor jungle, the better.

Stone Age wisdom on . . . the environment we live in

- Many of us have become distanced from the natural environment that was our home, constant backdrop and source of sustenance for millennia.
- Make nature a daily habit, remembering that this is a necessity not a luxury, scheduling in regular time outdoors.
- Dress for outdoor success, investing in clothes that are warm and waterproof, enough to encourage you to spend time outdoors in all seasons.
- Try new nature-focused pursuits such as forest bathing.
- When in the city, identify places where you can find regular sanctuary and peace.
- Bring the 'round world' into your home, embracing greenery, organic shapes and natural materials.

13

Ritual and Rites

Maharashtra, western India. A man stands on top of a shrine, looking down at a sea of upturned faces fifty feet below. He holds in his arms a baby, wide-eyed and oblivious. The man holds out his arms and drops the baby over the edge, sending it falling through the air. Seconds later the infant bounces, safely, onto a sheet held outstretched by several men. The practice of dropping babies off tall buildings was practised in parts of India for around seven hundred years. Although outlawed, it's reported that some parents still submit their children to this ordeal in the belief that it will ensure their good health: vaccination via vertigo.

Wherever you go in the world you will find people performing dangerous, strange and nonsensical rituals. In Indonesia, members of the Dani tribe grieve a loved one by cutting the top of their finger off. In Germany, the *Polterabend* ritual has the family of a newly-wed couple smashing a small mountain of porcelain in their home for good luck. In Papua New Guinea, the Kaningara people cut their skin to look like crocodile scales. In

Denmark, turning twenty-five can mean being doused in water and sprinkled with cinnamon by your family.

The roots of ritual run deep in the human story. In the Tsodilo Hills of the Kalahari Desert in Botswana, archaeologists discovered a huge, carved stone python in a cave, its sides pockmarked – and thousands of burned spear heads, which had been brought from hundreds of miles away. No other signs of habitation were found. What had been going on there? The answer, archaeologists reckon, is that 70,000 years ago this was the site of the first known human ritual.[1]

Many mysterious finds from prehistory have no rational explanation. There's the fossilised human faeces which contained the remains of a whole venomous snake, including its fang.[2] There are the carved snake heads found in what is now Ukraine.[3] There are the mysterious stone circles fashioned by Neanderthals in the Brunuqiel caves of south-west France around 175,000 years ago. There is the vast temple-like site at Göbekli Tepe in Turkey, an 11,000-year-old creation of elaborately decorated stone circles, built thousands of years before Stonehenge. Again and again, prehistoric mysteries can only be explained as remnants of ritual.

What drove them to such efforts? What were they doing carving elaborate snakes or hauling massive stones around when their business was survival? The answer must be that human beings have long felt an instinctive need to perform rituals – but why?

Ritual for reassurance

I knocked on the door of the semi-detached suburban house reluctantly. In my late twenties, Friday nights were for getting drunk on vodka and Coke, not for having dinner with a family I didn't even know. The occasion was my first Shabbat meal: the Jewish Friday night dinner. I was interviewing the mother of the family for another project, and she had asked me to come along. It might be the dullest couple of hours ever, but how could I refuse?

The door opened to a house alive with jollity and numerous relatives. Sandwiched between two uncles on a sofa, I was given a brief lesson in the steps of the evening: the lighting of the candles; the sipping of the kiddush wine; the shuffling into the kitchen to wash our hands; the silence after the washing; the breaking of the bread. One uncle informed me of his 'most important rule' of Shabbat: 'never, ever leave hungry'. Despite myself, I was moved by it all; by the atmosphere, the cosiness, the *care* taken: wine goblets polished and white cloths starched as though this were not just a family meal but a five-star event.

Saying goodbye and stepping into the winter night, the cold felt not just literal but metaphorical. From that cosy scene I was going back to a life punctuated by the odd birthday booze-up but which was otherwise ritual-free. I was envious of my hosts. What a gift: to have that weekly ritual to anchor your life. Whatever troubles came your way, there would always be the candles, the kiddush wine, the conversation.

This predictability is a major reason why we are drawn to ritual. When the world is capricious, it is order and familiarity we yearn for. In 1912 the poet Rupert Brooke was 'sweating, sick and hot' in Berlin when he wrote his yearning-for-home masterpiece 'The Old Vicarage, Grantchester', which ends with the lines ' . . . stands the church clock at ten to three? | And is there honey still for tea?'[4] In troubled times, he yearned for the English ritual of afternoon tea, its silver teaspoons anchors of familiarity in a turbulent world.

Rituals ground and reassure us, which is why many sports stars do odd things to prepare for a big performance. Before each serve, the tennis player Rafael Nadal taps the floor with his foot, wipes his nose, and tucks his hair behind his left ear, then his right. He has described these rituals as 'a way of putting my head in order'.[5] While some have mocked Nadal for these quirks, there's wisdom in them: scientists have found that engaging in rituals can actually help performance by decreasing anxiety.[6]

Like Nadal, some hunter-gatherers turn to ritual to improve their performance. Before they set out on a day's hunt, !Kung men stack several leather discs on their upturned left palm, blowing on them before throwing them on a piece of cloth. These 'runes' are read by a diviner who will give them clues about how the hunt will pan out. It might seem like superstitious nonsense, but if for thousands of years this ritual has stiffened sinews before the hunt, doesn't it make a kind of sense?

Ritual for bonding

Rituals don't just calm us; they bond us. At twelve years old I enjoyed a brief obsession with Arsenal football club. I had an Arsenal pencil-case, the kit, a team scarf studded with badges. A dozen times I travelled to the ground in North London to see them play, ready to sing 'Ian WRIGHT, WRIGHT, WRIGHT' at the top of my lungs. The curious thing, in retrospect: I wasn't *that* into football. I didn't even know the rules. What intoxicated me was being alongside thousands of other people in a stadium, all chanting in unison. When the ball hit the back of the net and 20,000 people erupted, my heart was on fire.

In 1912 the sociologist Émile Durkheim coined the expression 'collective effervescence' to describe the kind of euphoria that arises when a group of people are involved in a ritual together: 'Once the individuals are gathered together, a sort of electricity is generated from their closeness.'[7] By inducing intense collective emotion, rituals bond people together like nothing else.

The ritual doesn't have to involve a cast of thousands, either. Neuroscientist Paul Zak attended a wedding where he took blood samples from the (very understanding) bride, groom, parents, relatives and friends before and after the ceremony. The blood was checked for levels of oxytocin, the bonding hormone. Unsurprisingly, the bride and groom experienced a surge in oxytocin – but so too did their parents, friends and relatives.[8] Ritual is, in short, an unrivalled bonding device.

The cost of lost rituals

Since the snake-carvers of the Stone Age, human beings have created rituals because they make us feel safe and calm, happy and connected. How, then, does it affect us when rituals start slipping away from our lives?

Mankind's major source of ritual has been religion, and across the Western world it is in decline. In the UK, more than half of all people describe themselves as having 'no religion'.[9] Whether you think this is a good thing or not, what is undeniable is that the retreat of religion has taken with it a lot of the rituals that punctuated lives and brought us together.

Collective spiritual celebrations are on the decline, as are coming-of-age rituals. While some countries do still have traditions such as the 'sweet sixteen' party in the US, or Japan's Seijin no Hi festival for twenty-year-olds, many parts of the modern world have no formal rites of passage at all. How was I initiated into adult life? Getting my ears pierced alone in a shopping centre at thirteen? Drinking vinegar-like wine on park benches with friends? Passing my driving test? In truth, there was no 'coming of age'. I slipped into adulthood without fanfare.

In the context of the human story, this is remarkable. Traditional societies have long thought it not only nice but *necessary* to mark the transition into adulthood. In Australian Aboriginal society, for example, Walkabout was a rite of passage that required boys in their early teens to live in the wilderness for up to six months.

Although we may find such rites of passage extreme, there does seem to be wisdom in recognising an individual's transition into manhood or womanhood. If formally marking the start of adult life makes young people feel that they have somehow earned their place in adult society, aren't they more likely to feel a healthy respect for that society, and for themselves?

Some have argued that the decline of rites of passage can lead to serious social problems, because when young people (particularly young men) are not given a formal transition into adult life, they fill the vacuum by making up their own, warped initiations: dabbling in crime or joining gangs. As the philosopher Roger Scruton put it, 'deprive young people of a rite of passage *into* the social order and they will look for a rite of passage *out* of it'.[10]

Adolescent rootlessness and even criminality are the sharpest symptoms of ritual's retreat. Beyond this, I would tentatively suggest a more widespread symptom: a vague sense of unfulfilment. 'Tentatively', because obviously this makes leaps. Many would argue that their lives are A-OK without any form of ritual. Many are proud of our enlightened, post-superstitious times in which we don't throw babies off buildings or cut off our fingers. Fair enough, but doesn't the ubiquity of ritual in some shape or form across every single human culture suggest that we *Homo sapiens* have a primal need for it? Might an absence of ritual therefore create a sense in many people that something is missing, even if they can't put their finger on what that something is?

THE PALEO PRESCRIPTION
Weave rituals into your life

I have a weakness for picture frames. Wood or metal, baroque or simple, it doesn't matter. I love their transformative power. Over the years I have put all sorts of not-very-special objects behind glass: broken tiles, feathers, old matchboxes. Once inside a frame with a thick white mount these objects magically turn into *art*. They take on new meaning and beauty because, once framed, they are asking to be looked at in a different way. Frames elevate the everyday – and rituals have the same effect.

Rituals are a frame that we can put around experiences to make them more meaningful and beautiful. It's easy for months to slip through our fingers like sands through the hourglass. One minute it's January, the next it's September; one minute you're nineteen, the next you're forty-three. Life moves fast. We can't stop the sands from falling, but by framing moments in our lives with ritual, we somehow *thicken* the time so that looking back we feel we have lived it and given texture to each passing week, month and year.

My ritual pick 'n' mix

For a long time I lived a life without much in the way of ritual, aside from the odd burst of 'Happy Birthday' and midnight mass on Christmas Eve. The more I learned about our species' need for ritual, the more I realised that I was missing out on a vital part of the human experience. I wanted more of the rhythms that punctuate so many lives around the world: more ceremony, more celebration, more 'collective effervescence'.

I set out to deliberately incorporate more ritual into my life. That has meant borrowing some rituals and building my own. For some, the idea of borrowing ritual from a religion that you don't practise or a culture you don't belong to might seem shallow. But non-believers have a long history of borrowing. You could argue that sitting in a yoga class is borrowing from Hinduism. Meditating is borrowing from Buddhism. Playing a sheep in the nativity play is borrowing from Christianity. Appropriating a culture's ritual might be wrong if you're denigrating it – but if you're *celebrating* it respectfully, what's the problem? Here are some of the rituals I've woven into my life.

The secular sabbath

The most important ritual I've borrowed is the idea of a weekly (secular) sabbath in which we focus on family, food and togetherness. Every Monday night is special: no work, no laptops, no telly. Certain elements are always the same. We play a game, light candles at the table, have a nice pudding we've made together. This isn't only inspired by the Jewish Shabbat. In the early 20th century, the leaders of the Church of Jesus Christ of Latter-day Saints suggested that church members should hold 'family home evenings'. A Mormon family interviewed about this said: 'Whether or not it's always a complete success ... it's important just that [the children] know that it's going to happen every week.'[11] I'm sure at some point my children will roll their eyes at our secular sabbaths, but whatever else happens in life, the Monday night anchor will always be there.

The spring swim

The renewing power of water is a feature in many religious rituals, from Christian and Sikh baptism to Muslim Wudu (washing hands before prayer). My own water-based ritual is the spring swim, welcoming the new season in late March or early April with an outdoor dip. Each year it's a different place; that's part of the ritual. I'll find a day when I have no duties or distractions, find a destination, pack and go. After the swim I'll think about what I want to get out of the spring and summer; a bit like New Year's resolutions, but for me it's better to make them in the hopeful light of spring.

Holly gathering

The first Sunday in December is our foraging day. Part one of the ritual is the home-made hot chocolate, flavoured according to taste: mint? Orange? Cinnamon? Part two is heading to the woods to gather the greenery. Everyone has a basket and a list of things to find: holly, ivy, fir ... Back at home we stick everything in green floristry foam to make wreaths, garlands and holly-covered objects for the table. It's an aesthetic disaster, but that's not the point.

Baby's first bath

I'd heard about a practice in Nigeria in which the grandmother gives a new baby its first bath, symbolising that the community will help to raise the child. A charming ritual – so I borrowed it. In a candle-lit bathroom my mother has given my babies their first bath, rubbing oil onto the baby afterwards and saying a prayer.

How to build a ritual

- Remember the aim: putting a frame around moments in life to make them more special, meaningful and memorable.
- Look to the months ahead: are there any junctions where you'd like to slow down, celebrate or mark something for yourself or others (beyond their birthday)? Is someone you care about changing jobs, recovering from an illness, marking an anniversary, moving house, trying a new challenge? What are the dates, seasons or occasions that you want to honour?
- Once you have an occasion to mark, think about the shape of your ritual. Remember the frame metaphor. You're putting a frame around a moment; there should be a clear beginning, middle and end.
- Think about the sensory layers of your ritual. Can you

---

include things that look attractive, that create awe, that are colourful, that smell evocative, that taste good?

- How can you make the ritual meaningful to whoever is involved? Saying a few words, lighting a fire, creating something, sharing something?
- There are no ritual police who will come for you if your ritual is not spiritual or outlandish enough. You don't have to don a shamanic headdress and ululate at the moon. It's about creating a nice event for yourself, your family or community that can be repeated, and that can take on richer meaning with each repetition.

Go for group fizz

In my early thirties, feeling adrift, I enrolled on an introduction-to-Christianity course at a big evangelical church in London. When the ten weeks were up I was so taken with the good and smiling people who ran it that I decided I would become a good and smiling person myself. For months I would head there every Sunday morning for sermons and heart-swelling music, enjoying a post-church high that would last at least until Tuesday.

Alas, though, I started to feel like a fraud. In truth, I wasn't devoted to Christ. My main motivation for attending was not worship but *community*; my voice joining hundreds of others in song, heart soaring to the vaulted ceiling. I was after the feeling of collective effervescence, or 'group fizz', as the author Jules Evans has put it.[12]

One evening I attended a service at which several people around me were overcome by the Holy Spirit, falling to the floor and crying out. Feeling a pressure to do *something* and not just stand there like a spiritless potato, I closed my eyes and ... pretended to speak in tongues. Aiming for Polish, I sounded more like the cartoon penguin Pingu. This was a spiritual low, after which I didn't set foot inside a church for over seven years. It was only during the quiet of the Covid lockdowns that I realised how much I missed the collective effervescence I had felt in church. As soon as restrictions on large gatherings started easing, I sought them out.

Sometimes, this means going to church, whether a raise-the-roof evangelical service or sober Catholic mass, but the 'group fizz' feeling doesn't only come from collective worship. Back in the 1990s I got my group fizz from Arsenal matches, as I mentioned earlier. In more recent years I've got my fix in the crowds at the coronation of King Charles III, shouting my heart out at Ascot's horse races along with thousands of others, 'Aaaahing' at the diamond blasts in the sky on fireworks night. Whether at concerts or sports matches or church services, there's nothing quite like feeling that synchronicity with a large group of people. It's worth seeking out.

Let's dance

One activity that inspires feelings of collective effervescence like no other is dancing. The shapes our ancestors threw haven't fossilised, but there's good evidence that dancing stretches way back in the human story. Cave art found in Borneo painted between 13,600 and 20,000 years ago shows a line of people with their legs bent, looking like Paleolithic line dancers.[13] In the Bhimbetka caves of India – where the rock art was made up to 30,000 years ago – two long lines of figures hold hands while a musician plays an instrument beside them. Today the San communities of the Kalahari do something called the 'trance dance', stamping their rattle-clad feet for hours, hyperventilating and working themselves into a transcendent state.

In every known human society, people have got down on the dance floor/cave floor. When you learn about the community-cementing benefits of dance, it's easy to believe that this has been a way of humans bonding since someone first knocked a lute out of an antler horn. Whether it's the hokey-cokey or a mass waltz, rituals that involve synchronised movement create what the historian William H. McNeill has called 'muscular bonding'.[14]

For ten or fifteen years I enjoyed this kind of collective effervescence once or twice a week in a nightclub. Now that I'm of an age where I am in no danger of being asked for ID at the door, I'd rather not go to clubs, but I realised it would be a personal tragedy not to dance regularly again. So, to seek this kind of group fizz, I've done various classes, from Latin dance to Lindy hop. Dancing is too life affirming to ditch as we get older. As the dance critic Edwin Demby put it, 'dance is a little insanity that does us all good', which is ritual in a nutshell.

A year of rituals

As well as building your own rituals, you might want to (respectfully) borrow them, inspired by the rich feast of rituals from different religions and cultures.

Spring

Tu Bishvat is a Jewish holiday celebrating the revival of nature and the planting of trees. Its secular version, 'Arbor Day', is celebrated around the world, with people coming together to plant trees in the spring.

Possibly the most beautiful ritual there is, **Holi** is a Hindu spring holiday in which a large number of people gather to throw coloured powder at each other: magenta, green and turquoise fly through the air. Many Holi festivals are open to the public.

The festival of **Hanami** is widely celebrated across Japan, as people go out for picnics to mark the coming of the cherry blossoms. If blossom doesn't feature near you, how about celebrating the coming of the daffodils, tulips or bluebells?

Summer

In the UK, the **summer solstice** falls in late June. Historically, pagans would light bonfires and dance the (shortest) night away. Some celebrate by watching the sun both rise and set on this longest day.

The Japanese **Obon** Festival is a three-day holiday held to honour the spirits of the dead. The graves of loved ones are cleaned and decorated, and celebrations held in their honour.

Autumn

One of the dates that seems to have slipped from widespread celebration in my lifetime is the **harvest festival**. Many food banks work in conjunction with local communities to arrange harvest collections and suppers for those who need the help – a good reason to give and get together.

Thanksgiving may be an American ritual – from pumpkin pie to turkey pardoning – but its central message of thankfulness celebrated with a sumptuous feast is an easy one to borrow.

Winter

In rural England, **wassailing** is the centuries' old practice of making a 'hullaballoo' in an orchard to ward off bad spirits and ensure a good harvest. On the twelfth night after Christmas (6 January) wassailers head among the apple trees to sing and drum their hearts out – and are rewarded with warm, spiced drinks. In England, several wassails are open to the public.

Burns Night suppers celebrate Scotland's national poet and are rich with rituals: songs, poems and 'toasting the haggis'. Given the huge Scottish diaspora, there are plenty of Burns Night suppers and events celebrated in towns and cities all over the world.

Stone Age wisdom on . . . rituals

- We've lost many of the rituals that gave human beings a sense of control and connection for hundreds of thousands of years.
- Resolve to mark holidays and special days more distinctly, with traditions and rituals that are repeated year after year.
- Take every opportunity to celebrate and mark the passing of time, from the turning of the seasons to milestones being hit.
- Seek out 'group fizz': collective experiences which stir the soul (such as concerts, sports matches or religious services).
- Dance more regularly, preferably in a group.

14

Me and Us

We live in an age of self-obsession, when people think nothing of taking pictures of their gym-honed navels and posting them on social media, when it's OK to proclaim your own uniqueness, when we ruminate endlessly on our own 'journey' and place in the world.

The world has long been divided, broadly, into two halves: the individualistic West and the collectivist East. In individualistic nations we tend to think that life is about pursuing our own happiness more than observing social obligations. We tend to value personal achievement over the success of the group.

How did this global split begin? Some argue it's to do with the way we organise our economies. Others say it's rooted in the medieval Catholic Church's mission to wipe out incest by banning cousin-to-cousin marriages, which had the unintended consequence of fragmenting communities.[1] Over the 20th century our tendency to see ourselves as being at the centre of the universe was strengthened by psychoanalysis and its emphasis on self-work; by parenting styles that encouraged children to think that the world revolved around them; and by politicians and thinkers who argued that individual rights mattered above all else.

One of the most influential of those thinkers was Ayn Rand. Born in St Petersburg in 1905, she was 12 when the October Revolution turned life upside down. Her father's pharmacy was nationalised and the family forced to flee. Unsurprisingly, this experience seeded a life-long loathing of communism. Rand went to the other extreme, becoming a champion of the idea that people should be free to pursue their own interests, however 'selfish' they may be. The hero of her novel *Atlas Shrugged* declares that man should exist 'for his own sake, and the achievement of his own happiness is his highest moral purpose'.

Over many decades this 'every man for himself!' rallying cry permeated the culture, from greed-is-good boardrooms to reality TV shows. In the second half of the 20th century, Westerners have become more and more self-obsessed. In 1963 just 12 per cent of adolescents agreed with the statement 'I am an important person'; by 1992 77–80 per cent did.[2] A review of American books published between 1960 and 2008 found that over time, the pronouns 'I' and 'me' were used more frequently than 'we' and 'us'.[3] Analysis of popular songs released between 1980 and 2007 show that 'words related to self-focus' increased.[4] Whitney Houston crooned about the importance of learning to love yourself – and many have clearly mastered the art.

The me-first myth

Some argue that the me-first mentality is just part of being human, that it runs through the story of *Homo sapiens* like letters through a stick of rock. In the 1600s, philosopher Thomas Hobbes argued that our hunter-gatherer ancestors were locked in a 'warre of every one against every one'.[5] Charles Darwin's survival-of-the-fittest theories left many believing that life has always been a dog-eat-dog slog. In this vision of how humans used to be, there was a lot of self-interest and little altruism.

It seems a sensible assumption, but it's wrong. For most of our time on earth, the emphasis wasn't on 'me' but on 'us'. Over and over again, when outside observers have come into contact with hunter-gatherers they have found them to be generous, fair, altruistic and cooperative. When Christopher Columbus discovered America's native population in 1492 he marvelled in a letter home: 'they are very simple and honest and exceedingly liberal with all they have, none of them refusing anything he may possess when he is asked for it. They exhibit great love toward all others in preference to themselves.'[6]

Anthropologist Christopher Boehm spent decades studying the data on 150 contemporary hunter-gatherer societies that (broadly speaking) live or lived as our Stone Age ancestors once did. In each and every case, the dominant values were generosity, cooperation and altruism.[7] And these societies didn't just cross their fingers and hope that everyone would get the sharing-caring memo. They had strategies to ensure that people stuck to it, shaming and expelling the selfish and the power-hungry, the hoarders and the egotists.

In hunter-gatherer societies, the self is surrendered to the good of the group. A glimpse of this modest mindset can be seen in the cave paintings of prehistory. Looking at hundreds of these paintings, I have been struck time and again by a question: where are the people? Beyond a few basic stick figures, humans barely feature. Why, when they were so talented at depicting lions, mammoths and rhinos, did these artists not create detailed images of people? Is it too much of a stretch to imagine that in the long era when solidarity was essential to survival, individuals themselves weren't deemed *that* important? As the prehistorian Jean Clottes has suggested, 'In the Paleolithic world, humans were not at the centre of the stage.'[8]

By putting 'us' before 'me', hunter-gatherers weren't being do-gooders. They *had* to have this mindset because cooperation was essential to survival. If you only looked out for number one, number one wouldn't last very long. You had to rely on others' generosity when times were hard. Ayn Rand might have sneered that 'It is only the inferior men that have collective instincts – because they need them', but even the best hunters might have come home empty-handed a few days in a row.[9] To survive the lean days, everyone needed to rely on their tribe mates to survive. You were each other's insurance policy.

(An aside: at the end of her life, living in the US and suffering from lung cancer, Rand accepted Social Security and Medicare to help with her spiralling medical bills. Having previously called those who used such systems 'parasites', in the end the go-it-alone hero enjoyed the benefits of mutual reliance.)

Why we moved from 'us' to 'me'

Because helping each other out was essential to survival for so long, our brains and bodies evolved to respond positively to altruistic behaviour. In one study, researchers hooked up over seventy preschool children to electrodes, which would measure their physiological responses. The kids then had to earn tokens that they could exchange for prizes. At the end, the researchers gave them a sob story about some 'ill children' who couldn't make the day: would they donate some of their tokens to get toys for the sick kids? According to the physiological data, the children who donated felt calmer and less stressed. For lead researcher Jonas Miller, this suggested that 'We might be wired from a young age to derive a sense of safety from providing care for others.'[10]

Here's a curiosity. If we're hardwired to cooperate, if being altruistic feels good, why are so many human beings so often so selfish? I think there are a number of reasons why mankind's focus has moved along the spectrum from 'us' towards 'me'. The first is that in our day-to-day lives, collaboration is not a life-or-death necessity any more. Broadly speaking, we work and earn money to feed ourselves independent of others. If reliance on the group is reduced, so too is the need for altruism.

Another reason we might be more self-centred is that we are not embedded in communities in the way we once were. While those who have always lived in the same place might be high-fiving half the people they pass on the street, many of us – such as those who have moved to a big city – don't belong to communities that can be described as 'tight-knit'. Technology has increased the distance between us. We spend more time alone. It's not easy to love thy neighbour in a meaningful way if you've only spoken to them over the street WhatsApp group.

When we're not around a wider community so much, a wider community isn't able to scrutinise our behaviour so much either. In his book *Tribe: On Homecoming and Belonging*, Sebastian Junger makes the point that 'subsistence-level hunters aren't necessarily more moral than other people; they just can't get away with selfish behaviour because they live in small groups where almost everything is open to scrutiny'.[11]

The impulse to behave when we're being observed runs deep. The 'watching eye effect' has found that when people are in the presence of images that depict eyes, they are more likely to behave altruistically. If just being pretend-watched by a picture of some eyes makes us act differently, this would suggest that the need to be approved of by the tribe still runs deep. But most of the time these days we're not *physically there* to police each other's selfishness or praise each other's altruism.

Self-absorption and sadness

What has the growing emphasis on 'me' done for our wellbeing? Has rampant please-yourself individualism meant widespread happiness? Hardly. Psychologist Dr Jean Twenge has spent thirty years studying huge data sets to work out how attitudes change between different generations, from the Silents (born 1925–45) to Gen Z (1995–2012), with the Baby Boomers (1946–64), Gen X (1965–79) and Millennials (1980–94) in between. From this 10,000-foot viewpoint, she has observed a marked increase in self-centredness.[12] By the time Millennials came of age, 'the individual self was not merely important, it was paramount'.

Twenge has found that as the self has taken centre stage, so depression and anxiety have soared. Generation Z are particularly miserable because the internet they are addicted to has turbo-charged darker aspects of individualism. Starting in the early 2010s (when smartphones were suddenly everywhere), depression, loneliness and self-harm increased sharply among adolescents in English-speaking countries such as the US, the UK and Canada. Social media is not only fuelling self-obsession but also making it more painful. On the one hand the culture is saying that you must strive to be special, not just a face in the crowd, on the other it's endlessly flaunting people whose talents, looks and lives seem more special than yours. Is it any wonder so many young people feel miserable?

THE PALEO PRESCRIPTION
Get over your self

Matthieu Ricard was raised in an affluent family in France. There he gained a PhD in cellular genetics before jacking it all in to become a Buddhist monk in the mountains of Nepal. According to researchers who scanned his brain and found remarkable levels of feel-good gamma waves, he is 'the world's happiest man'. With his combination of Western intellectualism and Eastern spirituality, it's fair to say that Ricard knows a bit about how to improve wellbeing – and for him, getting over yourself is key: 'Inner freedom ... is won only by minimizing obsessive self-absorption.'[13]

Humans' shift from us-focused to me-focused has been framed as a kind of enlightenment: isn't it great that these days we know our worth, know our rights, are tuned in to what we need and want? Self-love, self-worth, self-esteem: all good things, yes? To a point. It's good not to loathe yourself, obviously. But the evidence also suggests that self-absorption is really bad for us. It can lead to anxiety.[14] It can set the conditions for depression.[15] A number of studies have shown that having a strong, clearly delineated sense of self is linked to fluctuating mood, whereas selflessness – meaning a weaker distinction between ourselves and others – is linked to what researchers call 'authentic-durable happiness'.[16]

Every day, I try to challenge the habit of egocentric thinking. When I start focusing too heavily on me, when my ego is stoked or I catch myself thinking how the great 'I' can conquer, achieve and show off, I check myself. Although I'll never reach Buddhist-levels of self-transcendence like Matthieu Ricard, here are some approaches I use to help shift focus from me, me, me to us.

Remember you're mortal

We've been taught that it's psychologically healthy to believe in our own specialness. 'Everyone's special' sang Barney the big purple dinosaur in the 1990s, and a generation of preschoolers (now adult Millennials) took this as a fact. I prefer the message given out by an English teacher named David McCullough, whose 2012 commencement address at a US high school went viral. His message: 'Do not get the idea you're anything special, because you're not.'

In today's culture this is a stark statement, but throughout human history people have known that there's value in pulling egos down if they're floating towards the stratosphere. When victorious Roman generals returned home and enjoyed a procession through the streets, a slave was employed to whisper in his ear: 'remember you are mortal'. Remember you're flesh and blood like the rest of us. Remember you'll be worm feed, too, one day. *Don't get above yourself, buddy.*

Similar tactics are used by hunter-gatherers. The anthropologist Christopher Boehm coined the phrase 'reverse dominance' to describe all the tactics they use to ensure no one thinks that they are better than the rest, such as ridiculing those who bring home a great feast from the hunt.[17] It's about forcibly grounding people for the sake of the group.

When I feel my ego start to inflate, or self-obsession rearing its head, I try some hunter-gatherer-inspired self-levelling. This doesn't mean fierce self-criticism (which is, after all, just another form of self-focus); rather, it's a gentle and humorous reminder that, to paraphrase David McCullough, 'you're nothing special, sweetie'.

Avoid your self

Mirrors, mirrors on the wall are such a feature of modern homes that we never reflect on the effect of looking in them all the time. Every time we gaze on our reflection we consider in split seconds both how we look and how others will perceive us. Mirrors remind us that we are a separate self, a 'something' to be scrutinised, praised or criticised.

It's so natural to gaze on ourselves multiple times a day, and yet so unnatural in the context of the human story. For most of our time on earth our own reflection didn't exist, unless a prehistoric Narcissus caught a glimpse of themself in a still lake. Might a feeling of connection with others have been more possible without this frequent reminder of our own distinct selves? Might the general absence of human figures in cave art be because they didn't frequently dwell on their appearance?

This is no proven theory, but I think that having too many mirrors around encourages self-absorption. For me, 'getting over your self' means getting rid of the mirrors. OK: I have a small mirror in my bathroom because applying lipstick with guesswork is a bad idea, but the rest of the house is mirror-free. The modern obsession with taking selfies is another sure-fire trigger for self-focus. I've never been a selfie-taker, but if I had been, this would be another self-reflective practice that I'd ditch.

Seek awe

For decades the primatologist Jane Goodall lived in the forests of Gombe National Park in Tanzania in order to observe the chimpanzees there. One morning, standing on a grassy ridge overlooking a lake, the sunlight broke through the clouds and sparkled on the green, glittering scene below. The awe that struck Goodall in that moment had a peculiar effect on how she felt about herself: 'It seemed to me, as I struggled afterward to recall the experience, that self was utterly absent.'[18]

Goodall's experience is similar to what has been called 'the small self effect'.[19] When people experience something awesome – like looking over Yosemite National Park – and are then asked to draw or depict themselves, they tend to make themselves look *smaller* than they otherwise would have done.[20] When exposed to awesome things, our sense of humility increases and arrogance decreases.[21] Awe's more extreme cousin, ecstasy, comes from the ancient Greek word *ekstasis*, meaning 'to be or stand outside oneself, a removal to elsewhere'.

When it comes to what inspires awe, we all have our poison: spiritual experiences, Beethoven's ninth, cloud-skimming skyscrapers. The most popular source of awe is nature. In the cartoon strip Calvin and Hobbes, Calvin declares 'Look at all the stars! The universe just goes out for ever and ever!' Hobbes's response: 'It kind of makes you wonder why man considers himself such a big screaming deal.' Nature puts us in our place. It reminds us of our insignificance in the wider scheme of things.

Our hunter-gatherer ancestors were treated to this perspective-altering experience every day. On wide-open savannahs, in majestic forests and on icy steppes they were constantly reminded that they weren't such a big screaming deal.

Awe is an awesome word in itself. I try not to get too hung up on whether I'm experiencing full-blown, slack-jawed awe. It's enough to switch my focus from self to the scene ahead for a while: looking up at forest canopies, standing on the edge of a vast sea. Every year in winter I try to make a couple of trips to the Somerset Levels to see the starling murmurations. Watching this speckled black mass swoop and soar against the blue is like having pure wonder injected into my veins.

Where to find awe

- Get into nature: observe the sea, the sky at night, vast lakes and distant horizons.
- Watch David Attenborough-style TV shows on nature, which absorb you in the wonders of the world.
- See incredible talents perform – dancers, footballers, singers, tennis players – whose skills you could never compete with and can only admire.
- Get lost in great art or music.
- Catch the sun rising or setting.

Putting 'us' first

Remember David McCullough, whose commencement address to students contained the salty reminder 'Do not get the idea you're anything special, because you're not'? Later he followed it up with this sweetener: 'The great and curious truth of the human experience is that selflessness is the best thing you can do for yourself.'

It is hard to make advice about serving others anything but saccharine, but it is a basic and proven truth that few things bring more happiness, meaning and comfort than serving 'us' rather than 'me'. A stack of research demonstrates it. In one experiment, participants had their brains scanned while they were presented with a long list of charities. In each case they had to choose whether to donate, or stick some cash into a reward account for themself. When they put others' needs before their own, the part of the brain associated with food and sex lit up.[22]

Being generous to others has been found to significantly lower blood pressure,[23] to increase longevity,[24] and to boost happiness. One experiment conducted in countries as wide-ranging as Canada, Uganda, India and Vanuatu found that people are happier spending $5 on other people than on themselves.[25]

Still, let's face it: knowing about the benefits of acting altruistically doesn't always compel us to do it. How can we weave selflessness into our lives? What practical steps can we make to push ourselves back along the spectrum from 'me' to 'us'?

Plan acts of kindness

In the 1970s, officials in Washington DC decided to hold a festival called Human Kindness Day. Thousands of people were to sing and sway in the sun, enjoying a spirit of neighbourliness. By evening the event had seen a shooting, over 200 robberies and 150 people treated in hospital. Years later a woman who had been a child at the time recalled: 'Dad was driving us through DC when a cop came up to our car and said, "Roll up your windows and lock your doors. It's Human Kindness Day."'[26]

Like organised fun, there is something ridiculous about the idea of *planned* kindness. Yet I've found that in a busy life, if I am to consistently weave selflessness into my days, I need to organise it. I need to challenge myself to do something selfless daily, or the intention gets knocked flat by the demands of children, chores and work.

I'm inspired by the random acts of kindness movement, which is all about doing something nice for someone you don't know very well – or a complete stranger. Years ago I was in the passenger seat of a friend's car, heading through a Starbucks drive-thru. We ordered our coffees and pulled up to the second window to pay. 'Too late.' The guy smiled. 'The woman in the car in front just settled your bill.' What? This completely floored me. We had no way of thanking her. It was completely random, and all the more powerful for it.

Acts of kindness don't have to involve money, or strangers. It could be a cup of tea ferried to a colleague, letting someone jump in the queue ahead of you, complimenting a stranger on their wonderful bag, giving a sandwich to the homeless guy, surrendering your seat on a crowded train, scraping the ice off your neighbour's windscreen once you've done your own. Tiny things; the work of seconds. A lot of people will do this kind of thing automatically many times a day. For more self-absorbed types like me, it helps to turn this into a regular practice. A happy by-product of these acts: just by thinking about how you can bring a little delight or comfort to someone else helps you get into their head – and out of your own.

Extend the boundaries of home

Next to the road leading up to my daughter's school there's a pathway, separated by a series of posts, which walkers and buggy-pushers use to stay safe from moving cars. When we returned to school last autumn the path was overgrown with thorns, thick tendrils snaking across the ground. Unable to get a buggy through it – and not wanting scratched legs – all the parents (including me) nipped out into the road for the few thorn-covered metres of path, rolling our eyes at each other in a way that said: *Can't they sort this out?*

A week later, walking to school for the afternoon pickup, I saw an elderly gentleman with gardening gloves on, two large buckets of thorns beside him. 'Ah, thank you,' I said, assuming he was from the council, 'we were hoping someone would come out ...' 'Not a problem,' he replied, smiling, 'I picked up my granddaughter yesterday ... it was a terrible mess, wasn't it?'

Oh. The exchange was chastening. Instead of thinking, like I had: *Can't someone sort this out?* and hoping for a faceless 'someone' to ride to the rescue, the man had done the job himself. This was *his* community, so *he'd* clear it up.

In modern, industrialised societies, our home – and our responsibility for maintaining it – ends firmly at our front door or front gate. But this strict delineation between what belongs to *me* and what belongs to *us* is a relatively new thing in the history of our species. For most of our time on earth we didn't have clear boundaries between our home and the outside world; the outside world *was* our home.

I'm trying to emulate the attitude of the man who cleared up the thorns from the pathway, to think of home not as my own four walls but the streets around me too. I'm not saying we should all be out tarmacking potholes, but where it's easy enough for us to help maintain our wider home – by litter-picking, for instance – why not do it? The benefits far outweigh the hassle. Home shouldn't end at our front door.

Find your cause

The world is loud with cries for help: on climate change, on the never-ending cycle of conflict, on the disease and starvation and injustice that afflict so many. The global perspective given to us by the news means that a lot of our us-focused energy can be absorbed by simply *despairing* about the state of the world, and not knowing what to do about it beyond tapping out an indignant tweet. Of course it's right for us to help our global neighbours however possible. But to help counter this feeling of powerlessness – and to focus our altruistic efforts – I also think it's a good idea to commit to a local cause that we care deeply about.

Hunter-gatherers' cooperative efforts were focused on a small tribe of people. They could see the difference they were making, which is a great motivator. It's a good idea, therefore, to find a local cause that inspires you – from saving the library to volunteering in the foodbank – and focus some of your altruistic energy on that.

Stone Age wisdom on . . . *getting over your self*

- Billions of us have been shaped by modern individualistic culture, which encourages us to reflect endlessly on ourselves – a major departure from the egalitarian approach of our ancestors.
- The shift from 'us' to 'me' is a significant cause of unhappiness, placing pressure on us to be unique and special.
- Try to avoid the seductive trap of self-absorption; avoid mirrors, selfies and self-aggrandisement on social media.

- To help break out of the introspective boxes that we have put ourselves in, experience awe whenever possible, losing yourself in admiration of something external to yourself.
- Plan small acts of kindness to shift your focus from your self on to others.
- Find a local cause that you care about in which to invest your time and energy, feeding the part of our Stone Age soul that craves altruistic effort.

Afterword

During the most difficult times of my life, when I was anxious and low – head-sick – I was also homesick. A lot of us in the modern world are homesick. We're yearning for the home our species was shaped in: a home of tight tribes, more equal societies, simpler relationships, fewer expectations, satisfying work, health-giving food, frequent movement, bountiful nature, proper leisure. The further 'progress' takes us away from all this, the more homesick we get.

As I wrote at the beginning of this book, so much of modern life is wonderful. Who would turn the clock back on clean water and communicating with people half a world away, on aeroplanes and access to the world's knowledge, on medicine and microwaves, on foreign restaurants and firework displays? The Paleo Life isn't about rejecting modern life, only those aspects of it which leave many of us dissatisfied and depressed.

So much of what makes us unhappy we simply submit to, as though 21st-century life comes as a job lot: the grim stuff thrown in with the glorious bits. But here's the point that I hope has come across: to a degree, we get to choose which parts of modern life we accept, and which we reject.

Sometimes we forget that we have that choice. The power of conformity is real, even for those of us who pride ourselves on being independent thinkers. In the 1950s a psychologist called Solomon Asch conducted experiments that revealed how much opinions are influenced by those around us. Participants were shown an image of a line, after which they had to pick its match from a series of other lines. When answering independently, it was simple enough to work out. Then Asch mixed things up, involving undercover participants who were in on the experiment. These actors declared the wrong answer, and something extraordinary happened. Even when the genuine participants *knew* the right answer, they went along with the opinion expressed by all the others. Conformity trumped reality.

The instinct to conform might be an evolutionary adaptation that helped to keep us on the right side of our prehistoric tribe, but it doesn't serve us today when it means swallowing whole all the worst ideas, trends and teachings of modern life. If you saw several cars ahead of you driving through a red traffic light you wouldn't follow them; you'd think they were crazy. And yet as a species we blindly follow each other through red lights that look like 'progress', knowing in our core that the direction is not the right one for us, whether that's the obsessive use of technology or empty consumerism.

I admit that I don't always succeed in rejecting the worst of modern life. I'll doom-scroll, I'll look for ego-flattery online,

I'll succumb to the urge to buy something I don't need. But if I fall off the tracks, I know how to get back on them to a lifestyle that's more simple, more streamlined, more human. The Paleo Life has clarified what makes me feel better and what makes me feel worse.

If you're giving any of the advice in this book a go, don't beat yourself up about sticking to exact diets or schedules. The last thing we modern humans need is another set of rules we can either fail or succeed at. This book is about relieving such pressures, not imposing them. Instead, I hope you've gleaned from these pages a few nuggets of Stone Age wisdom to help you identify the aspects of modern life that aren't working for you. I hope it helps you to clarify what matters. Above all, I hope it takes you closer to a place that feels like home.

Acknowledgements

This book leans heavily on the work of countless anthropologists, archaeologists, evolutionary psychologists, scientists, historians and thinkers. It is impossible to mention them all, but I have been particularly inspired by the work and words of: Jared Diamond, James Suzman, Sarah Blaffer Hrdy, Daniel Everett and Robin Dunbar.

Much of their work would have been impossible without the forbearance of all the hunter-gatherers who agreed to have their lives observed, their hearts monitored, their happiness measured and their habits probed. It's thanks to their tolerance of all this that we in the WEIRD world can glimpse another way of life.

I am so grateful to those who have been supportive of this project. To my agent Joanna Swainson, whose enthusiasm has been infectious; to Hana Murrell, for getting *The Paleo Life* in the hands of readers around the world; to Jillian Young, for her positivity and clear sense of direction; and to all the team at Piatkus/ Little, Brown who have helped to polish the book. Thanks also to Barley and Liz for their encouraging words.

On the home front, thank you, Sean, for making me pakoras, and making me laugh. Thanks to my children for not destroying my laptop more than once in the writing process. I am grateful above all to my mum, whose interest in my prattling for the past forty-odd years helped me believe that I have something worth saying.

References

Introduction: The Progress Paradox

1. For rise in depression see: Liu, Q., He, H., Yang, J., Feng, X., Zhao, F. and Lyu, J., 'Changes in the global burden of depression from 1990 to 2017: Findings from the Global Burden of Disease study', *Journal of Psychiatric Research*, 126 (2020), 134–40, doi: 10.1016/j.jpsychires.2019.08.002. For rise in anxiety see: Yang, X., Fang, Y., Chen, H., Zhang, T., Yin, X., Man, J., Yang, L. and Lu, M., 'Global, regional and national burden of anxiety disorders from 1990 to 2019', *Epidemiology and Psychiatric Sciences*, 6 (2021), 30–6, doi: 10.1017/S2045796021000275

2. McManus, S., Bebbington, P., Jenkins, R. and Brugha, T. (eds), 'Mental health and wellbeing in England: Adult psychiatric morbidity survey 2014' (published 2016)

3. Ibid.

Chapter 1: Meet the Hunter-Gatherers

1. Hobbes, T., *Leviathan* (1651, Chapter XIII)
2. Diamond, J., 'The Worst Mistake in the History of the Human Race', *Discover Magazine*, 1 May 1999, pp. 95–8
3. Pandit, T. N., *The Sentinelese* (Seagull Books, 1990, pp. 24–25)
4. Biswas-Diener, R., Vittersø, J. and Diener, E., 'Most people are pretty happy, but there is cultural variation: The Inughuit, the Amish, and the Maasai', *Journal of Happiness Studies*, 6 (2005), 205–26
5. Martin, R. J. and Cooper, A. J., 'Subjective well-being in a remote culture: The Himba', *Personality and Individual Differences*, 115 (2017), 19–22
6. Minkin D. and Reyes-García, V., 'Income and wellbeing in a society on the verge to market integration: The case of the Tsimané in the Bolivian Amazon', *Journal of Happiness Studies*, 4 (2017), 993–1011, doi: 10.1007/s10902-016-9756-7
7. Frackowiak, T. and Oleszkiewicz, A., et al., 'Subjective happiness among Polish and Hadza people', *Frontiers in Psychology*, 11 (2020), 1173, doi: 10.3389/fpsyg.2020.01173
8. Everett, D., *Don't Sleep, There Are Snakes* (Profile Books, 2009)
9. James Suzman interviewed by Michaeleen Doucleff for NPR, published online 1 October 2017

Chapter 2: Tribe and Friendship

1. Shultz, S., Opie C. and Atkinson, Q. D., 'Stepwise evolution of stable sociality in primates', *Nature*, 479 (2011), 219–22, doi: 10.1038/nature10601. PMID: 22071768

2. Eisenberger, N. I., Lieberman, M. D. and Williams, K. D., 'Does rejection hurt? An FMRI study of social exclusion', *Science*, 302 (2003), 290–2, doi: 10.1126/science.1089134

3. Kross, E., Berman, M. G. and Mischel, W., et al., 'Social rejection shares somatosensory representations with physical pain', *Proceedings of the National Academy of Sciences*, 108 (2011), 6270–5, doi: 10.1073/pnas.1102693108

4. Xia, N. and Li, H., 'Loneliness, social isolation, and cardiovascular health', *Antioxidants & Redox Signaling*, 9 (2017), 837–51, doi: 10.1089/ars.2017.7312

5. Kraav, S., Lehto, S. M. and Kauhanen, J., et al., 'Loneliness and social isolation increase cancer incidence in a cohort of Finnish middle-aged men', *Psychiatry Research*, 299 (2021), doi: 10.1016/j.psychres.2021.113868

6. Umberson, D. and Karas Montez, J., 'Social relationships and health: A flashpoint for health policy', *Journal of Health and Social Behaviour*, 51 (2010) 54–66, doi: 10.1177/0022146510383501

7. Detillion, K. E., Craft, T. K. S. and Glasper, E. R., et al., 'Social facilitation of wound healing', *Psychoneuroendocrinology*, 8 (2004), 1004–11, doi: 10.1016/j.psyneuen.2003.10.003

8. According to recent surveys by Data Reportal and Statista, approximately 60 per cent of the global population is on social media, spending an average of 151 minutes a day on social-media sites

9. McCormick, T. H., Salganik, M. J. and Zheng, T., 'How many people do you know?: Efficiently estimating personal network size', *Journal of the American Statistical Association*, 489 (2010), 59–70, doi: 10.1198/jasa.2009.ap08518

10. Navarro, H., Miritello, G., Canales, A., et al., 'Temporal patterns

behind the strength of persistent ties'. *EPJ Data Science,* 6 (2017), doi: 10.1140/epjds/s13688-017-0127-3

11. Dunbar, R. I. M., 'Neocortex size as a constraint on group size in primates', *Journal of Human Evolution,* 22/6 (1992), 469–63, doi: 10.1016/0047-2484(92)90081-J

12. Dunbar, R. I. M., *Friends: Understanding the Power of our Most Important Relationships* (Little, Brown, 2021)

Chapter 3: Hierarchy and Status

1. In 1954, psychologist Leon Festinger put forward his influential social comparison theory, which suggests that humans have an innate need to judge their own abilities against others. Many subsequent studies have revealed the emotional cost of social comparison. See, for instance, Tesser, A., Millar, M. and Moore, J., 'Some affective consequences of social comparison and reflection processes: The pain and pleasure of being close', *Journal of Personality and Social Psychology,* 54/1 (1988), 49–61, doi: 10.1037/0022-3514.54.1.49; or Kohler, M. T., Turner, I. N. and Webster, G. D., 'Social comparison and state-trait dynamics: Viewing image-conscious Instagram accounts affects college students' mood and anxiety', *Psychology of Popular Media,* 10/3 (2021), 340–9, doi: 10.1037/ppm0000310

2. Takahashi, H., et al., 'When your gain is my pain and your pain is my gain: Neural correlates of envy and schadenfreude', *Science,* 323/5916 (2009), 937–99, doi: 10.1126/science.1165604

3. Lee, Richard B., 'Eating Christmas in the Kalahari', *Natural History Magazine,* December 1969

4. Sahlins, M., *Stone Age Economics* (Routledge, 1972, pp. 1–40)

5. Suzman, J., *Affluence Without Abundance* (Bloomsbury Publishing, 2017, p. 16)

6. Mazur, P. M., *American Prosperity: Its Causes and Consequences* (Viking Press, 1928, pp. 24–5)

7. Wilson, O., 'Shoppers eye view of ads that pass us by', experiment featured in the *Guardian*, 19 November 2005

8. Michel, C., Sovinsky, M., Proto, E. and Oswald, A., 'Advertising as a major source of human dissastisfaction: Cross-national evidence on one million Europeans', in Rojas, M. (ed.), *The Economics of Happiness*, Springer (2019), pp. 217–39

9. Longfellow, H. W., 'Suspiria', *The Complete Poetical Works of Henry Wadsworth Longfellow* (e-artnow, 2020, p. 191)

Chapter 4: News and Views

1. BBC News article: 'Londoner solves 20,000-year Ice Age drawings mystery', 5 January 2023

2. Miller, G. A., 'Informavores', in Machlup, F. and Mansfield, U. (eds), *The Study of Information: Interdisciplinary Messages* (Wiley-Interscience, 1983, pp. 111–113)

3. Kobayashi, K. and Hsu, M., 'Common neural code for reward and information value', *Proceedings of the National Academy of Sciences* (2019), doi: 10.1073/pnas.1820145116

4. Samuelson, L.H., *Some Zulu Customs and Folk-lore*, The Church Printing Co., 1905

5. The world population at the time of writing is 7.88 billion Population estimates of prehistoric times vary widely: one study suggests that around 130,000 years ago the human population was between

100,000 and 300,000. For this calculation I have used the upper estimate: 300,000 people. See Sjodin, P., et al., 'Resequencing data provide no evidence for a human bottleneck in Africa during the penultimate glacial period', *Molecular Biology and Evolution*, 29/7, 1851–60, doi: 10.1093/molbev/mss061

6. Trussler, M. and Soroka, S. 'Consumer demand for cynical and negative news frames', *International Journal of Press/Politics*, 19/3, (2014), 360–79

7. Hanson, R., *Hardwiring Happiness* (Penguin Random House, 2013, p. 27)

8. Heinlein, R.A., *Stranger in a Strange Land* (Hodderscape, 2007)

9. Holman, E. A., Garfin, D. R. and Silver, R.C., 'Media's role in broadcasting acute stress following the Boston Marathon bombings', *Psychological and Cognitive Sciences*, 111/1 (2013), 93–8

10. For 9/11, see: Ahern, J. and Galea, S., et al., 'Television images and probable post-traumatic stress disorder after September 11: The role of background characteristics, event exposures, and perievent panic', *Journal of Nervous and Mental Disease*, 192/3 (2004), 217–26, doi: 10.1097/01.nmd.0000116465.99830.ca

For Sichuan earthquake, see: Yeung, N. C. Y. and Lau, J. T. F., et al., 'Media exposure related to the 2008 Sichuan earthquake predicted probable PTSD among Chinese adolescents in Kunming, China: A longitudinal study', *Psychological Trauma: Theory, Research, Practice, and Policy,* 10/2 (2018), 253–62

For Ebola, see: Garfin, D. R., and Holman, E. A., et al., 'Media exposure, risk perceptions, and fear: Americans' behavioral responses to the Ebola public health crisis', *International Journal of Disaster Risk Reduction*, 77 (2022), doi: 10.1016/j.ijdrr.2022.103059

For Paris 2015, see: Robert, M. and Stene, L. E., et al., 'Media exposure and post-traumatic stress symptoms in the wake of the November 2015 Paris terrorist attacks: A population-based study in France', *Frontiers in Psychiatry*, 12 (2021), doi: 10.3389/fpsyt.2021.509457

11. Van Bavel, J., Brady, W. J., Wills, J. A. and Jost, J. Y., 'Emotion shapes the diffusion of moralized content in social networks', *Proceedings of the National Academy of Sciences*, 114/28 (2017), 7313–8

Chapter 5: Work and Leisure

1. *The Influencer Report: Engaging Gen Z and Millennials*, Morning Consult, 2019

2. Lee, R. B., *The !Kung San: Men, Women and Work in a Foraging Society* (Cambridge University Press, 1979)

3. Lambert, K., *Lifting Depression: A Neuroscientist's Hands-on Approach to Activating Your Brain's Healing* (Basic Books, 2008, pp. 47–69)

4. Keynes, J. M., 'Economic possibilities for our grandchildren', published in *Essays in Persuasion* (Harcourt Brace, 1932, pp. 358–73)

5. Dyble, M. and Thorley, J., et al., 'Engagement in agricultural work is associated with reduced leisure time among Agta hunter-gatherers', *Nature Human Behaviour*, 3 (2019), 792–6

Chapter 6: Body and Movement

1. Babyak, M. and Blumenthal, J. A., et al. 'Exercise treatment for major depression: Maintenance of therapeutic benefit at 10 months', *Psychosomatic Medicine*, 62 (2000), 633–8. See also Blumenthal,

J.A., et al., 'Effects of exercise training on older patients with major depression', *Archives of Internal Medicine*, 159/19 (1999), 2349–56, doi: 10.1001/archinte.159.19.2349

2. Sandercock, G. R. H., Moran, J. and Cohen, D. D., 'Who is meeting the strengthening physical activity guidelines by definition: A cross-sectional study of 253 423 English adults', *PLoS ONE*, (2022), doi: 10.1371/journal.pone.0267277

3. From the Active Lives adult study 2022, which tracked the activity of 175,000 respondents in England for a year; for all Active Lives studies, see Sport England's archives at sportengland.org

4. O'Keefe, J.H. and Vogel, R., et al., 'Achieving hunter-gatherer fitness in the 21st century: Back to the future', *American Journal of Medicine*, 123/12 (2010), 1082–6, doi: 10.1016/j.amjmed.2010.04.026

5. Raichlen, D.A., et al., 'Physical activity patterns and biomarkers of cardiovascular disease risk in hunter-gatherers', *American Journal of Human Biology*, 29/2 (2017), doi: 10.1002/ajhb.22919

6. Marlow, F. W., 'Hunter-gatherers and human evolution', *Evolutionary Anthropology*, 14 (2005), 54–67

7. According to the National Travel Survey 2019, in which 14,356 people were interviewed. Shown on statista.com

8. Sands, R. and Sands, L., *The Anthropology of Sport and Human Movement: A Biocultural Perspective* (Lexington Books, 2012, p. 268)

9. Johansson, E., et al., 'Sitting, standing and moving during work and leisure among male and female office workers of different age: A compositional data analysis', *BMC Public Health*, 20/1 (2020), 826, doi: 10.1186/s12889-020-08909-w

10. Ng, S.W. and Popkin, B., 'Time use and physical activity: A shift away from movement across the globe', *Obesity Review*, 13 (2012), 659–80

References

11. Raichlen, D.A. and Pontzer, H., et al., 'Sitting, squatting, and the evolutionary biology of human inactivity', *Proceedings of the National Academy of Sciences*, 117/13 (2020), 7115–21, doi: 10.1073/pnas.1911868117

12. Pontzer, H., et al., 'Locomotor anatomy and biomechanics of the Dmanisi hominins', *Journal of Human Evolution*, 58 (2010), 492–504. See also Trinkaus, E., 'Squatting among the Neanderthals: A problem in the behavioural interpretation of skeletal morphology', *Journal of Archaeological Science*, 2 (1975), 327–51

13. Hewes, G.W., 'World Distribution of Certain Postural Habits', *American Anthropologist*, 57/2 (1955), 231–44

14. Pontzer, H., et al., 'Energy expenditure and activity among Hadza hunter-gatherers', *American Journal of Human Biology*, 27/5 (2015), doi: 10.1002/ajhb.22711

15. Kaplan, H., et al., 'Coronary atherosclerosis in indigenous South American Tsimané: A cross-sectional cohort study', *Lancet*, 389, (2017), 1730–9

16. Liu, W., et al., 'Current understanding of coronary artery calcification', *Journal of Geriatric Cardiology*, 12/6 (2015), 668–75, doi: 10.11909/j.issn.1671-5411.2015.06.012

17. Ryan, T.M and Shaw, C.N., 'Gracility of the modern *Homo Sapiens* skeleton is the result of decreased biomechanical loading', *Proceedings of the National Academy of Sciences*, 112/2, (2015), 372–7, doi: 10.1073/pnas.1418646112

18. Herman Pontzer interviewed for article 'Staying fit isn't a New Year's resolution for these hunter-gatherers', featured on npr.org, 3 January 2017

19. All referenced in Currey, M., *Daily Rituals: How Artists Work* (Knopf, 2013)

20. Lee, I. M. and Paffenbarger, R. S., 'Associations of light, moderate, and vigorous intensity physical activity with longevity', *American Journal of Epidemiology*, 151/3 (2000), 293–9, doi: 10.1093/oxfordjournals.aje.a010205.

21. Pes, G.M., et al., 'Nutrition related to male longevity in Sardinia: An ecological study', *Nutrition, Metabolism and Cardiovascular Diseases*, 23/3 (2013), 212–9, doi: 10.1016/j.numecd.2011.05.004

22. Diaz, K.M., et al., 'Patterns of sedentary behaviour and mortality in U.S. middle-aged and older adults', *Annals of Internal Medicine*, doi: 10.7326/M17-0212

Chapter 7: Feast and Fast

1. Rauber, F., et al., 'Ultra-processed foods and excessive free sugar intake in the UK: A nationally representative cross-sectional study', *BMJ Open*, 9/10 (2019), doi: 10.1136/bmjopen-2018-027546

2. Research study of 2,400 British families conducted by Lisa Heggie of University College London, presented to the European Congress on Obesity in Maastricht in 2022

3. DiFeliceantonio, A. G., et al., 'Supra-additive effects of combining fat and carbohydrate on food reward', *Clinical and Translational Report*, 28/1 (2018), 33–44, doi: 10.1016/j.cmet.2018.05.018

4. Zohar, I., Alperson-Afil, N., Goren-Inbar, N., et al., 'Evidence for the cooking of fish 780,000 years ago at Gesher Benot Ya'aqov, Israel', *Nature Ecology and Evolution*, 6 (2022), 2016–28, doi: 10.1038/s41559-022-01910-z

5. Marriotti Lippi, M., et al., 'Multistep food plant processing at Grotta Paglicci (Southern Italy), around 32,600 cal B.P', *Proceedings of the*

National Academy of Sciences, 112/39 (2015), 12075–80, doi: 10.1073/pnas.1505213112

6. Arranz-Otaegui, A., et al., 'Archaeobotanical evidence reveals the origins of bread 14,400 years ago in northeastern Jordan', *Proceedings of the National Academy of Sciences*, 115/31 (2018), 7925–30, doi: 10.1073/pnas.1801071115

7. See Mattson, M.P., *The Intermittent Fasting Revolution* (MIT Press, 2022)

8. Mummert, A., Esche, E., Robinson, J. and Armelagos, G.J., 'Stature and robusticity during the agricultural transition: Evidence from the bioarchaeological record', *Economics & Human Biology*, 9/3 (2011), 284–301, doi: 10.1016/j.ehb.2011.03.004

9. Smith, W., 'The teeth of ten Sioux Indians', *Journal of the Anthropological Institute of Great Britain and Ireland*, 24 (1895), 109–116, doi: 10.2307/2842212

10. Merrill, B.D., et al., 'Ultra-deep sequencing of Hadza hunter-gatherers recovers vanishing gut microbes', *bioRxiv*, (2022), doi: 10.1101/2022.03.30.486478

11. Spector, T., 'I spent three days as a hunter-gatherer to see if it would improve my gut health', article published on theconversation.com, 30 June 2017

12. Quoted in Bodley, J.H., *Victims of Progress* (Rowman & Littlefield, 2014, p. 173)

13. O'Keefe, S., Li, J., et al., 'Fat, fibre and cancer risk in African Americans and rural Africans', *Nature Communications*, 6/article number 6342 (2015), doi: 10.1038/ncomms7342

14. For more on the interaction between sugar and leptin, see Lustig, R., *Fat Chance: The Hidden Truth about Sugar, Obesity and Disease* (Fourth Estate, 2014)

15. Healy-Stoffel, M. and Levant, B., 'N-3 (omega-3) fatty acids: Effects on brain dopamine systems and potential role in the etiology and treatment of neuropsychiatric disorders', *CNS and Neurological Disorders – Drug Targets,* 17/3 (2018), 216–32, doi: 10.2174/1871527317666180412153612

Chapter 8: Sleep and Rest

1. Ekirch, R., *At Day's Close: A History of Night-time* (Weidenfeld & Nicolson, 2006)

2. Samson, D. R., et al., 'Chronotype variation drives night-time sentinel-like behaviour in hunter-gatherers', *Proceedings: Biological Sciences*, 284 (2017), 1858, doi: 10.1098/rspb.2017.0967

3. Pegoraro, M., et al., 'Gene expression associated with early and late chronotypes in drosophila melanogaster', *Frontiers in Neurology,* 6 (2015), doi: 10.3389/fneur.2015.00100

4. Yetish, G., et al., 'Natural sleep and its seasonal variations in three pre-industrial societies', *Current Biology*, 25/21 (2015), 2862–8, doi: 10.1015/j.cub.2015.09.046

5. Piosczyk, H., et al., 'Prolonged sleep under Stone Age conditions', *Journal of Clinical Sleep Medicine*, 10/7 (2014), 719–22, doi: 10.5664/jcsm.3854

6. De la Iglesia, H. O., et al., 'Access to electric light is associated with shorter sleep duration in a traditionally hunter-gatherer community', *Journal of Biological Rhythms*, 30/4 (2015), 342–50, doi: 10.1177/0748730415590702

7. Boivin, D., Duffy, J. and Kronauer, R., et al., 'Dose-response relationships for resetting of human circadian clock by light', *Nature*, 379 (1996), 540–2, doi: 10.1038/379540a0

Chapter 9: Sex and Attraction

1. Smith, K. M. and Olkhov, Y. M., et al., 'Hadza men with lower voice pitch have a better hunting reputation', *Evolutionary Psychology*, 15/4 (2017), doi: 10.1177/1474704917740466

2. Beall, A. T. and Tracy, J. L., 'Women are more likely to wear red or pink at peak fertility', *Association for Psychological Science*, 24/9 (2013), 1837–41, doi: 10.1177/0956797613476045

3. Lewis, D. M. G., et al., 'Lumbar curvature: A previously undiscovered standard of attractiveness', *Evolution and Human Behaviour*, 36/5 (2015), 345–50, doi: 10.1016/j.evolhumbehav.2015.01.007

4. Cormier, Z., 'Gene switches make prairie voles fall in love', *Nature*, 2 June 2013, doi: 10.1038/nature.2013.13112

5. Larkin, P., 'Annus Mirabilis', *High Windows* (Faber and Faber, 1974)

6. Ibid.

7. Dr Helen Fisher interviewed in *Glamour* magazine, 26 May 2020. See also Dr Fisher's TED talk, 'The Brain in Love'

8. See Professor Maslar's book *Men Chase, Women Choose: The Neuroscience of Meeting, Dating, Losing Your Mind, and Finding True Love* (Vibrance Press, 2016)

9. Grisel, J., *Never Enough: The Neuroscience and Experience of Addiction* (Scribe UK, 2019)

Chapter 10: Love and Relationships

1. Survey conducted by YouGov.com on 17–18 May 2015, finding that 20 per cent of British adults asked if they had ever had an affair said yes (76 per cent said no, the rest preferred not to say)

2. Collins, H. K., Hagerty, S. F., Quoidbach, J. and Wood Brooks, A., 'Relational diversity in social portfolios predicts well-being', *Proceedings of the National Academy of Sciences*, (2022), doi: 10.1073/pnas.2120668119

See also Cheung, E. O., Gardner, W. L. and Anderson, J. F., 'Emotionships: Examining people's emotion-regulation relationships and their consequences for well-being', *Social Psychological and Personality Science*, 6/4 (2015), 407–14, doi: 10.1177/1948550614564223

3. Lippman, J. R., Ward, M. L. and Seabrook, R. C., 'Isn't it romantic? Differential associations between romantic screen media genres and romantic beliefs', *Psychology of Popular Media Culture*, 3/3 (2014), 128–40, doi: 10.1037/ppm0000034

4. Holmes, B., 'In search of my "one and only": Romance-related media and beliefs in romantic relationship destiny', *Electronic Journal of Communication*, 17/issue 3/4 (2007)

5. See Lieberman, D. and Long, M., *The Molecule of More: How a single molecule in your brain drives love, sex, and creativity – and will determine the fate of the human race* (BenBella Books, 2018)

6. Christie, A., *Poems* (London: William Collins and Sons, 1973, p. 124)

7. Ocobock, C. and Lacy, S., 'Woman the hunter: The physiological evidence', *American Anthropologist* (2023) doi: 10.1111/aman.13915

8. Gottman, J., *The Seven Principles for Making Marriage Work* (Orion Books Ltd, 2000, p. 28)

Chapter 11: Parenting and Children

1. Hrdy, S. B., *Mothers and Others* (Harvard University Press, 2009, p. 67)

2. Ivey, P., 'Cooperative reproduction in Ituri forest hunter-gatherers: Who cares for Efé infants?', *Current Anthropology*, 41, 856–66

3. Sear, R. and Steele, F., et al., 'The effects of kin on childhood mortality in rural Gambia', *Demography*, 39 (2002), 43–63

4. Morelli, G. A., and Tronick, E. Z., 'Efé multiple caretaking and attachment' in Gewirtz, J. L. and Kurtines, W. M. (eds), *Intersections with Attachment*, Lawrence Erlbaum Associates, 1991, 41–51

5. Chaudhary, N. and Swanepoel, A., 'What can we learn from hunter-gatherers about children's mental health? An evolutionary perspective, *Journal of Child Psychology and Psychiatry*, 64/10 (2023), 1522–5, doi: 10.1111/jcpp.13773

6. Gillis, J. R., *A World of Their Own Making: Myth, Ritual, and the Quest for Family Values* (Harvard University Press, 1997)

7. Diamond, J., *The World Until Yesterday* (Penguin Books, 2012, p. 187)

8. Ibid. p. 191

9. Ibid. p. 184

10. Salali, G. D., Chaudhary, N., Bouer, J., et al., 'Development of social learning and play in BaYaka hunter-gatherers of Congo', *Scientific Reports*, 9/article 11080 (2019), doi: 10.1038/s41598-019-47515-8

11. Diamond, J., *The World Until Yesterday* (Penguin Books, 2012, p. 198)

12. The findings from the Rouffignac caverns was presented at a Cambridge University conference on the archaeology of childhood in 2011, reported in various outlets, e.g.: 'Stone Age toddlers had art lessons', *Guardian*, 30 September 2011

13. Harlow, H., Dosworth, R. O. and Harlow, M. K., 'Total social isolation

in monkeys', *Proceedings of the National Academy of Sciences*, 54/1 (1965), 90–7, doi: 10.1073/pnas.54.1.90

14. González, C., *Kiss me! How to raise your children with love* (Pinter & Martin Ltd, 2012)

Chapter 12: Town and Country

1. United Nations Population Fund report: *State of World Population 2007*, p.11

2. Klein Goldewijk, K., Beusen, A. and Janssen, P., 'Long-term dynamic modelling of global population and built-up area in a spatially explicit way', *Holocene*, 20/4 (2010), 565–73, doi: 10.1177/0959683609356587

3. Peen, J., et al., 'The current status of urban-rural differences in psychiatric disorders', *Acta Psychiatrica Scandinavica*, 121/2, (2010), 84–93, doi: 10.1111/j.1600-0447.2009.01438.x

4. Sundquist, K., Frank, G. and Sundquist, J., 'Urbanisation and incidence of psychosis and depression: Follow-up study of 4.4 million women and men in Sweden', *British Journal of Psychiatry*, 184/4, (2004), 293–8, doi: 10.1192/bjp.184.4.293

5. Krabbendam, L. and Van Os, J., 'Schizophrenia and urbanicity: A major environmental influence – conditional on genetic risk', *Schizophrenia Bulletin*, 31/4 (2005), 795–9, doi: 10.1093/schbul/sbi060

6. Lederbogen, F., Kirsch, P. and Haddad, L., et al., 'City living and urban upbringing affect neural social stress processing in humans', *Nature*, 474 (2011), 498–501, doi: 10.1038/nature10190

7. Sundquist, K., Frank, G. and Sundquist, J., 'Urbanisation and incidence of psychosis and depression: Follow-up study of 4.4 million women

and men in Sweden', *British Journal of Psychiatry*, 184/4 (2004), 293–8, doi: 10.1192/bjp.184.4.293

8. Werneck, A. O. and Silva, D. R., 'Population density, depressive symptoms, and suicidal thoughts', *Brazilian Journal of Psychiatry*, 42/1 (2020), 105–6, doi: 10.1590/1516-4446-2019-0541

9. Lewis, J., 'As well as words: Congo Pygmy hunting, mimicry, and play', in Botha, R. and Knight, C. (eds), *The Cradle of Language* (Oxford University Press, 2009), doi: 10.1093/oso/9780199545858.003.0013

10. Hansell, A., Cai, Y. S. and Gulliver, J., in Harrison, R. M. and Hester, R. E. (eds), *Environmental Impacts of Road Vehicles: Past, Present and Future* (The Royal Society of Chemistry, 2017, pp. 107–32)

11. Dzhambov, A.M., 'Long-term noise exposure and the risk for type 2 diabetes: A meta-analysis', *Noise Health*, 17/74 (2015), 23–33, doi: 10.4103/1463-1741.149571

12. Münzel, T., Gori, T., Babisch, W. and Basner, M., 'Cardiovascular effects of environmental noise exposure', *European Heart Journal*, 35/13 (2014), 829–36, doi: 10.1093/eurheartj/ehu030

13. Orban, E., et al., 'Residential road traffic noise and high depressive symptoms after five years of follow-up: Results from the Heinz Nixdorf Recall Study', *Environmental Health Perspectives*, 124/5 (2016), 578–85, doi: 10.1289/ehp.1409400

14. Wilson, E.O., *Biophilia* (Harvard University Press, 1984)

15. James, P., Hart, E. J., Banay, R. R. and Laden, F., 'Exposure to greenness and mortality in a nationwide prospective cohort study of women', *Environmental Health Perspectives*, 124/9 (2016), 1344–52, doi: 10.1289/ehp.1510363

16. Andersen, L., Corazon, S. S. and Stigsdotter, U.K., 'Nature exposure

and its effects on immune system functioning: A systematic review', *International Journal of Environmental Research and Public Health*, 18/4 (2021), 1416

17. Weinstein, N., et al., 'Seeing community for the trees: The links among contact with natural environments, community cohesion, and crime', *BioScience*, 65/12 (2015), 1141–53, doi: 10.1093/biosci/biv151

18. Ulrich, R. S., 'View through a window may influence recovery from surgery', *Science*, 224/4647 (1984), 420–1, doi: 10.1126/ science.6143402

19. See Klepeis, N. E., et al., 'The National Human Activity Pattern Survey (NHAPS): A resource for assessing exposure to environmental pollutants', published in 2001 by the Lawrence Berkeley National Laboratory

20. Longfellow, H. W., 'Sunrise on the Hills', *The Complete Poetical Works of Henry Wadsworth Longfellow* (e-artnow, 2020, p.17)

21. Furuyashiki, A., et al., 'A comparative study of the physiological and psychological effects of forest bathing (Shinrin-yoku) on working age people with and without depressive tendencies', *Environmental Health and Preventative Medicine*, 24/1 (2019), 46, doi: 10.1186/ s12199-019-0800-1.

    See also Barbieri, A., Barbieri, G. and Donelli, D., 'Effects of forest bathing (shinrin-yoku) on levels of cortisol as a stress biomarker: A systematic review and meta-analysis', *International Journal of Biometeorology*, 63/8 (2019), 1117–34, doi: 10.1007/ s00484-019-01717-x.

    And Li, Q., 'Effect of forest bathing trips on human immune function', *Environmental Health and Preventative Medicine,* 15/1 (2020), 9–17, doi: 10.1007/s12199-008-0068-3.

And Ideno, Y., et al., 'Blood pressure-lowering effect of Shinrin-yoku (Forest bathing): A systematic review and meta-analysis', *BMC Complementary Medicine and Therapies*, 17/1 (2017), 409, doi: 10.1186/s12906-017-1912-z

Chapter 13: Ritual and Rites

1. Coulson, S., Segadika, P. and Walker, N., 'Ritual in the hunter-gatherer/early pastoralist period: Evidence from Tsodilo Hills, Botswana', *African Archaeological Review*, 33/2 (2016), 205–22

2. Sonderman, E. M., Dozier, C. A. and Smith, M. F., 'Analysis of a coprolite from Conejo Shelter, Texas: Potential ritualistic viperous snake consumption', *Journal of Archaeological Science: Reports*, 25 (2019), 85–93

3. Kotova, N., Kiosak, D., Radchenko, S., and Spitsyna, L., 'Microscopic examination of Mesolithic serpent-like sculptured stones from southern Ukraine' *Antiquity*, 92/366 (2018), doi: 10.15184/aqy.2018.249

4. Brooke, R., 'The Old Vicarage, Grantchester', *Delphi Complete Works of Rupert Brooke* (Delphi Classics, 2013)

5. Rafael Nadal quoted in an interview with Italian newspaper *Corriere Della Sera* in 2020

6. Hobson, N. M., Bonk, D. and Inzlicht, M., 'Rituals decrease the neural response to performance failure', *PeerJ* (2017), doi: 10.7717/peerj.3363

7. Durkheim, E., *The Elementary Forms of the Religious Life* (George Allen & Unwin Ltd, 1915, p. 215)

8. Detailed by the bride, Linda Geddes, in *New Scientist* magazine, 10 February 2010

9. British Social Attitudes Survey, 2016

10. Scruton, R., *Riots of Passage*, 11 October 2011, published by the American Enterprise Institute; https://www.aei.org/articles/riots-of-passage/

11. Interviewed as part of the American Families of Faith Project, led by Dollahite, D. C., and Marks, L. D of Brigham Young University. See americanfamiliesoffaith.byu.edu

12. Evans, J., 'Can governments create "collective effervescence" in their citizens? And should they?', *History of Emotions Blog* (emotionsblog. history.qmul.ac.uk; 20 March 2015)

13. Aubert, M., Setiawan, P., Oktaviana, A. A., et al., 'Palaeolithic cave art in Borneo', *Nature*, 564 (2018), 254–7, doi: 10.1038/s41586-018-0679-9

14. McNeill, W.H., *Keeping Together in Time: Dance and Drill in Human History*, Harvard University Press, 1995

Chapter 14: Me and Us

1. Schulz, J. F., Bahrami-Rad, D., Beauchamp, J. P. and Henrich, J., 'The Church, intensive kinship, and global psychological variation' *Science*, 366 (2019), 6466, doi: 10.1126/science.aau5141

2. Newsom, C. R., Archer, R. P., Trumbetta, S. and Gottesman, I. I., 'Changes in adolescent response patterns on the MMPI/MMPI-A across four decades', *Journal of Personality Assessment*, 81/1 (2003), 74–84, doi: 10.1207/S15327752JPA8101_07

3. Twenge, J. M., Campbell, W. K. and Gentile, B., 'Changes in pronoun use in American books and the rise of individualism, 1960–2008', *Journal of Cross-Cultural Psychology*, 44/3 (2013), 406–15, doi: 10.1177/0022022112455100

4. DeWall, C. N., et al., 'Tuning in to psychological change: Linguistic markers of psychological traits and emotions over time in popular

References

U.S. song lyrics', *Psychology of Aesthetics, Creativity, and the Arts*, 5/3
(2011), 200–7, doi: 10.1037/a0023195

5. Hobbes, T., *Leviathan* (Cosimo Classics, 2009, p. 72)

6. Taken from a letter from Christopher Columbus to Lord Raphael
   Sanchez, Treasurer to Ferdinand and Isabella, King and Queen of
   Spain, in Ford, P. L. (ed.), *Writings of Christopher Columbus: Descriptive
   of the Discovery and Occupation of the New World*, (C. L. Webster, 1892,
   pp. 33–51)

7. Boehm, C., *Moral Origins* (Basic Books, 2012)

8. Clottes, J., *What is Palaeolithic Art? Cave Paintings and the Dawn of
   Human Creativity* (University of Chicago Press, 2016)

9. Rand, A., journal entry on 22 February 1937, in Harriman, D. (ed.),
   Journals of Ayn Rand, New American Library, 1999

10. Miller, J. G., Kahle, S., Hastings, P. D., 'Roots and benefits of costly
    giving: Children who are more altruistic have greater autonomic
    flexibility and less family wealth', *Psychological Sciences*, 26/7 (2015),
    1038–45, doi: 10.1177/0956797615578476

11. Junger, S., *Tribe: On Homecoming and Belonging* (HarperCollins, 2016,
    p. 28)

12. Twenge, J. M., *Generations* (Atria Books, 2023)

13. Ricard, M., *Happiness: A Guide to Developing Life's Most Important Skill*
    (Atlantic Books, 2015, p. 208)

14. Gaydukevych, D. and Kocovski, N. L., 'Effect of self-focused attention
    on post-event processing in social anxiety', *Behaviour Research and
    Therapy*, 50/1 (2012), 47–55

15. Nakajima, M., Takano, K. and Tanno, Y., 'Adaptive functions of
    self-focused attention: Insight and depressive and anxiety symptoms',
    Psychiatry Research, 249 (2017) 275–80, doi: 10.1016/j.psychres.2017.01.026

16. Dambrun, M., 'Self-centeredness and selflessness: Happiness correlates and mediating psychological processes', *PeerJ* (2017), doi: 10.7717/peerj.3306

17. Boehm, C., *Hierarchy in the Forest* (Harvard University Press, 1999)

18. Goodall, J., *Reason For Hope: A Spiritual Journey* (Grand Central Publishing, 2004)

19. Bai, Y., et al., 'Awe, the diminished self, and collective engagement: Universals and cultural variations in the small self', *Journal of Personality and Social Psychology*, 113/2 (2017), doi: 10.1037/pspa0000087

20. Ibid.

21. Stellar, J.E., et al., 'Awe and humility', *Journal of Personality and Social Psychology*, 114/2 (2017), 258–269

22. Moll, J., et al., 'Human fronto-mesolimbic networks guide decisions about charitable donation', *Proceedings of the National Academy of Sciences*, 103 (2006), 15623–8, doi: 10.1073/pnas.0604475103

23. Whillans, A.V., et al., 'Is spending money on others good for your heart?', *Health Psychology*, 35/6 (2016), 574–83, doi: 10.1037/hea0000332

24. Brown, S.L., et al., 'Providing social support may be more beneficial than receiving it: Results from a prospective study of mortality', *Psychological Science*, 14/4 (2003), 320–7, doi: 10.1111/1467-9280.14461

25. Aknin, L. B., Dunn, E. W. and Willans, A. V., 'The emotional rewards of prosocial spending are robust and replicable in large samples', *Psychological Science*, 31/6, 536–45, doi: 10.1177/09637214221121100

26. Quoted in *Washington Post* article, '1975 Human Kindness Day's Cruel Violence', published 4 September 2011